UNCLE JACK

UNCLE JACK

Tony Williams

with Humphrey Price

ORION

First published in 2005 by Orion Books Ltd

Orion House, 5 Upper Saint Martin's Lane, London WC2H 9EA

1 3 5 7 9 10 8 6 4 2

The authors and publishers are grateful to Llyfrgell Genedlaethol Cymru/
The National Library of Wales for permission to reproduce photographs

A CIP catalogue record for this book is available
from the British Library.

ISBN-13 9 780752 867083
ISBN-10 0 752 86708 3

Printed and bound in Great Britain by
Clays Ltd, St Ives plc

www.orionbooks.co.uk

Tony:
*For my family for their support and patience
during my research and writing of this book.
To my brother for getting me started.*

Humphrey:
*With thanks to my parents for their advice and
support during the writing of this book.*

Acknowledgements

We would like to thank John Saddler, our agent, for his helpful and wise advice all through the process of researching and writing this book, our editors Stacey Hartman and Lucinda McNeile, and our publisher Alan Samson, for their support and incisive judgement.

Although we carried out a large amount of the research individually, for the sake of simplicity we have used 'we' throughout the book. We would both like to thank the people who assisted us in our various searches.

List of Illustrations

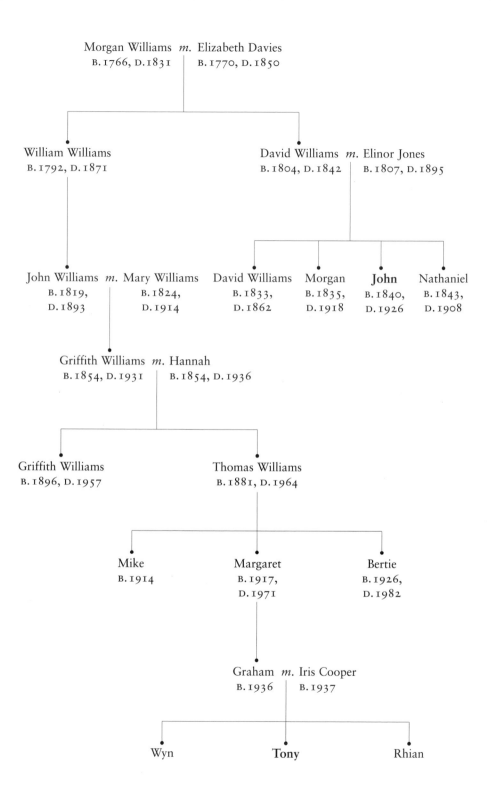

Morgan Williams *m.* Elizabeth Davies
B.1766, D.1831 | B.1770, D.1850

William Williams
B.1792, D.1871

David Williams *m.* Elinor Jones
B.1804, D.1842 | B.1807, D.1895

John Williams *m.* Mary Williams
B.1819, | B.1824,
D.1893 | D.1914

David Williams
B.1833,
D.1862

Morgan
B.1835,
D.1918

John
B.1840,
D.1926

Nathaniel
B.1843,
D.1908

Griffith Williams *m.* Hannah
B.1854, D.1931 | B.1854, D.1936

Griffith Williams
B.1896, D.1957

Thomas Williams
B.1881, D.1964

Mike
B.1914

Margaret
B.1917,
D.1971

Bertie
B.1926,
D.1982

Graham *m.* Iris Cooper
B.1936 | B.1937

Wyn

Tony

Rhian

Prologue

I grew up knowing very little about Uncle Jack, but then two things happened, almost in the same month, that started me off on this detective trail. I was always aware of my grandmother's great-great-uncle, even though he died in 1926 long before I was born. She would tell us stories about him when we went to stay with her as children. Family meant a great deal to my grandmother. She would tell us what a great man he was and that he had become a famous doctor with a London practice, how he had attended the royal family, had travelled in the tropical islands, and donated his collection of books to the National Library of Wales. He was always referred to as 'Uncle Jack' in the family, since that was how my grandmother had always known him.

The first indication that I was related to someone with a past worth looking into came at a launch party for a friend's new book. I was talking to my friend when a man came up to speak to her. He was neatly dressed, and looked every inch an academic; distinguished, with glasses, and scrupulously polite. He was greeted warmly by Iris, who then turned to me and asked if we'd met. We both said no, so she introduced us properly. His name was Brinley Jones, Dr Brinley Jones, and he was the President of the National Library of Wales. What an opportunity, I thought; I mentioned that I had written some books, and that I was interested in researching more about one of my relatives. 'Of course,' he said. 'I'm not certain, but I'm sure we have your books in the library.' He went on to say some nice things about my books. He then asked me who I was researching. 'Oh,' I said. 'He was an uncle, long dead. I think he had something to do with the foundation of the library, though I've no idea what. His name was John Williams.'

It was as if a light had been turned on. Dr Brinley Jones became very animated: 'John Williams? *The* John Williams? Well, do you know the history of the library? No? The National Library of Wales exists because of John Williams. And he's a relative of yours? We've not had a visit from one of his relatives in ages. You must come and visit us at the library. We have an extensive archive of his personal effects and papers, you know, and of course there's the collection of books he gave to the library. Nearly thirty thousand books altogether.'

I was astonished. So when exactly did he establish the library? I thought I knew something about him from the family stories, but I didn't know about this.

Dr Brinley Jones suggested I come to visit the library in Aberystwyth, together with any of my family who would like to see the collection they held, and they would show us the papers. He also invited us to stay for lunch.

The other thing that happened was this. My brother Wyn, knowing that my interest in the life of John Williams had recently grown, came to see me one evening, bringing with him a small box he had inherited from our grandmother, a parcel of items that had belonged to Uncle Jack. He had done what we all do when we receive things of this sort from relatives – he'd put it straight into the attic and forgotten all about it. Some years later, knowing that I'd become interested in the family's past, he thought that I would like to see it. He brought it over to my house so we could look at the parcel together. 'Here's Uncle Jack's box, that Nanny left me.' Wyn took the small parcel out from under his arm and placed it on the table in the kitchen, and we left it there while we had tea with my wife Cathy, and talked a little about what we could both remember from our childhood about our Nan.

Growing up on the edge of a quiet Welsh valley, my family had lived in a small village built along the side of a mountain riddled with old mines. One morning we woke up to find that the street just six doors away from our house had vanished into a large hole which had opened up in the ground. We went to have a look; it was black, down as far as you could see. We would drop stones down it, but you couldn't hear them land. Some time afterwards, everyone was moved away by the council. We moved to another village, near to the Black Mountains; a few years later my parents split up, and we all went in different directions while my mother tried to sort things out.

Wyn went to live with our grandmother. She lived in the same village, but slightly further down the valley. She shared the house with her brother, Bertie, who had never married. While he was alive, she had also looked after their father, Thomas, whose house it was originally and who had died back in 1964. Though Thomas died when I was about three years old, Nanny would only discuss John Williams with Wyn in a hushed undertone, as even then, criticism of the man was considered not the done thing within our family.

Wyn and I didn't talk about my great-great-uncle that often, but that night we chatted about what we had been told about him. Wyn knew the stories that had been passed down through the family, and added to the little I'd remembered. Uncle Jack had grown up on a farm, raised only by his mother after his father had died when Jack was two; then he had become a great doctor, done good and ground-breaking things at hospitals in London, and ended up as a doctor to the royal family, invited to Sandringham and Balmoral. Not bad for a lad from the hillsides of Carmarthen to be strolling the corridors of royal palaces. But Wyn knew more than I did, because, as an older child, he had been able to understand more of the stories when he'd heard them.

'Do you remember Nanny saying much more about Uncle Jack as a person?' I asked him, once the kids had cleared away tea and drifted back to watch TV or to finish their homework.

Wyn looked over at me, and paused while he considered.

'Well, she used to say a few things about him, but never very much. You know she was very proud of him. She said he was quite a distant man, not an easy man to be around as a child. You know why she was proud of him, what with him being friendly with the Queen and everything.'

Wyn paused. I could see that he was thinking back to a time when none of us was happy, as the quarrels between my mother and my father were acrimonious when we were young. I had not had a close relationship with my dad when we were little, but Wyn was older than me, and perhaps he knew more about what our old man was like then.

I thought I would try prompting Wyn's memory for him with some thoughts of my own. 'I remember much less about Nanny's house than you do. I remember that it had a warm and welcoming atmosphere when you came in, and then there was the smell of those clove sweets she liked to suck in the living room.'

Wyn smiled at the memory. 'I remember some good conversations with her in that living room. Mind you, she'd always wait till we were alone before she spoke about Uncle Jack.'

'Why?' I asked.

'Well, it was because she didn't want her father Thomas to overhear. It was about Uncle Jack's marriage, really. His wife died some time in the First World War, and nobody liked to bring it up anymore, but it had been an unhappy marriage. They'd had no children, and there was a suggestion that he'd had a relationship with a girl he shouldn't have – a servant or something. I don't know her name. It had caused a lot of upset within the family, apparently; Nanny knew this because she was told by her mum, Janet. But it was taboo to speak of it when Bertie or Daddy was around.'

We sat quietly for a few moments while we thought about marriages breaking up, and how that seemed to run in our family. Wyn spoke first:

'Right, then, Tony, are we going to look at this package?'

What did I expect to find when we opened it? Thinking back now, the hairs on the back of my neck start to rise as I remember how things began to take shape, giving me an indication that there was more to the story than I could possibly have imagined. At the time, though, there was no great transforming moment; no rush of cold air. No, all that came out was a stack of papers and old photographs. You know the kind of thing – letters written in an unfamiliar scrawl, hard to read because of the style of handwriting common then; sepia prints of people with unlikely hats and an abundance of facial hair, standing in front of brand new buildings that had long ago fallen down. The grim realisation of who Uncle Jack could have been didn't dawn upon me then, but only over the next few days as I started gradually to piece together the story of John Williams.

I don't remember what I picked up first – probably a photograph. I certainly can't remember what scene it showed. It took me a while before I picked up the letter that was to change everything.

The letter was short, and with no return address printed on it. There was Uncle Jack's writing; more recognisable than in any formal letter or note I had seen so far. His was a personal letter, addressed to someone called Morgan, and nothing in it was very revealing. It simply said that he was sorry that he couldn't come to a dinner one evening, as he had to be in Whitechapel to attend a clinic.

Whitechapel. I glanced at the year at the top of the letter – 1888. What was he doing in Whitechapel in 1888? Who was Morgan? I simply placed the letter in the pile next to me, said nothing, and went on to the next one.

I didn't even mention it to Wyn – it didn't seem worthwhile. I wasn't hiding the note – I just couldn't see what interest it would have been to him. Everyone knew I was the one who liked to discover things about the past. It wasn't that no one else cared, it's just that I was the one who was passionate about our family history.

The evening ended, and Wyn went home, with the small package of John Williams's effects now left for me to look over on the kitchen table. When he had gone, I went back inside, and picked up this letter again. Whitechapel? 1888?

The following week, I went to see Dr Brinley Jones. The National Library of Wales is an imposing, even intimidating, building. With landscaped gardens in front of it, and huge arched windows on either wing of the edifice, it has been made to look very much a symbol of the age it was created in. Authoritative and daunting, it stands like a benign parent overseeing the squabble of small houses in the city of Aberystwyth below it.

Dr Brinley Jones greeted me warmly, and showed me up to his office, where he'd laid out some of the precious items donated to the library by John Williams. It was an interesting display – some of the first books ever printed in Wales among them – but it was Sir John's life that I was far keener to talk about, and Dr Brinley Jones was only too happy to tell me what he knew. He explained that, after becoming a successful doctor in London, my great-great-uncle returned to Wales and devoted himself to establishing the National Library. He'd collected Welsh books and manuscripts all his life, and it was these that formed the main part of the library's collection when it was first established. Dr Brinley Jones also explained that it was Sir John's money that had helped the library with its lavish building plans.

I was amazed. I had always known, and half-remembered the stories, about my great-great-uncle's eminence, and now this was made literally concrete for me in the form of the National Library. I had had no idea about his work, but without my relative this building would probably not have existed. Dr Brinley Jones could see that I was mightily impressed, and suggested that I came back another day to have a look at Sir John's personal archives. 'We have masses of papers, letters, photographs and even medals that belonged to him,' he said to me. 'It will be nice to think they can come out of storage to be looked at by a relative.'

On our way out, he took me to see Sir John's statue. We walked through the cavernous hallway, with its exhibition stands showing recent work by Welsh artists, past glass-fronted bookcases and through the double doors to the main reading room, where, his back to the enormous arched windows overlooking the city, Sir John's marble statue rests. The man himself sits nine feet high, turning to his right as if disturbed from his thoughts by some noisy readers. In his left hand, he clutches papers etched with the plans of the completed library. He frowns into the reading room and at the people below him, his back set against the open world behind him, as a king might survey his private kingdom. In truth, I learned from my visit, the National Library of Wales was Sir John's kingdom. Not only was he the chief benefactor at its inception, he was also the driving force behind its establishment. No one is more deserving of this pride of place than John Williams.

Dr Brinley Jones shook my hand at the top of the steps outside the library, smiling and waving at me as I went back to my car. I made an appointment to come the following week and see the materials he mentioned. I was glad to step into the warm sunshine; a shiver ran down my back as I walked away from the library. I thought how funny Wyn would think it when I told him how much the National Library thought of our ancestor, what with the statue, and the portraits on show. He would be amused by the complete lack of interest in Uncle Jack shown by his own family. I turned around, and looked back up at the library; this huge building, that I'd never known about before now, only in existence because of him. I thought about this all the way down the hill, and all the way back home.

Chapter One

Like libraries everywhere these days, the security procedures at the National Library are draconian, but I dealt with that quickly enough and, a week later, carrying my notepad and pencil – you cannot even take a pen in – walked through to the manuscripts room. Quite a few people were working on their laptop computers, so, instead of silence, there was the incessant clicking of keyboards as the readers noted whatever treasures they had found. Overhead, a closed circuit TV camera slowly panned, monitoring my every move.

All of Sir John's papers are carefully catalogued in the library, so the first thing I did on arrival was to take down the red cloth-bound volume containing this catalogue and start to work through all the listings. It begins with the vast quantity of books that he donated to the library, all in Welsh, some dating as far back as the fifteenth century. They took him years to collect, and form the basis of the library's extensive collection of books published in Wales. The titles did not mean very much to me, but as this was the reason that the library stood where it did – and why I was there – I thought I should read through carefully.

The whole collection contains many thousands of volumes, including 120 items from the sixteenth century. The library's blurb read as follows:

Sir John Williams was an avid and intelligent collector of art and literature, and with the opening of the National Library he donated his collection of 25,000 books to the new institution. Among his most important donations were the first three Welsh books to be printed in 1546 and 1547, William Salesbury's New Testament of 1567 (in Welsh), William Morgan's Bible of 1588 (arguably the most important book ever in Welsh) and *Drych Cristionogawl* of 1587, which was the first book to be printed in Wales. From the Library of Hengwrt-Peniarth (which Sir John bought) the greatest treasures of the Welsh language were presented to the National Library. They are the Black Book of Carmarthen which includes the earliest Welsh poetry, *Llyfr Taliesin* (which includes the Welsh mythology, the *Mabinogi*), the Laws of Hywel Dda (the indigenous Welsh laws which date from the tenth century) and the famous Hengwrt copy of the work of Geoffrey Chaucer, *The Canterbury Tales*. Many of these priceless books are to be seen in the Library's permanent exhibition, *A Nation's Heritage*.

The praise for his collection continues:

It has a wide subject range but is mainly of Welsh interest. It also includes most of the Kelmscott Press publications and a large Arthurian collection, including the 1488 edition of *Lancelot du lac*; ephemera; chapbooks, almanacs, ballads, Civil War tracts.

I thought to myself, on reading these lists, that this collection, made up of the heritage of his homeland, represented Sir John Williams's future to him, not his past. This, and the building I sat in, was his memorial. I skipped through these pages, which fill some two thirds of the large book, intending to return to them in a more leisurely way later on, and made a start on the personal papers. There is only so much you can learn from the leftovers of someone's life; what you can learn starts at the beginning, so I started there. His private papers ran to over two hundred pages, covering not only documents, and photographs, but also miscellaneous objects. This list was invaluable during my time in the library, as it was carefully divided into sections, enabling me to follow hunches quickly through the archive. By far the longest section was to do with the royal family, and consisted of annotated lists of photographs and letters that marked the growth of the relationship between Uncle Jack and, astonishingly, Queen Victoria.

I turned to the first item on the top of the list, and started to read through. Countless items seemed to be catalogued in small detail; but I painstakingly read through everything, one item at a time, waiting for something to spring out and catch my attention. It took a while before I came across something interesting, and over halfway through the list. I had ploughed through pages of notes about letters, lists of personal effects, and clippings from turn-of-the-century newspapers. And then, on page 186, in the midst of notes about diaries that Sir John and his wife kept, I saw it, in entry 329, the first hint of something strange:

Diary of Sir John Williams for 1888. Most of the pages are missing; those that remain are blank.

There was that date again. What was going on here? And why would you keep a diary if the pages had been removed?

I set off for the reading room, and took down from the open shelves an encyclopaedia of dates and events. I turned to the page for 1888 where one entry read, 'In London's Whitechapel, from August to November, Jack the Ripper murdered five prostitutes.'

I felt numb. Whitechapel. That letter from John to Morgan. The diary. I went along the shelves, searching for a more comprehensive reference book.

In 1888, I read, five women were killed on the streets of Whitechapel by Jack the Ripper. He killed the women quickly and cleanly, and then, with the skill of a surgeon, removed from some of them their reproductive organs. The first victim was Mary Ann Nichols, killed on Friday, 31 August in Buck's Row, age forty-three. Buck's Row is now known as Durward Street. The second victim was Annie Chapman, who was found in Hanbury Street, on Saturday, 8 September. She was buried in Manor Park, and was forty-nine. Elizabeth Stride died next; she was forty-four and from Sweden. Known as Long Liz, she was found in Dutfield's Yard, Berner St (now Henriques St), on Sunday, 30 September. That same night, Catherine Eddowes was killed in Mitre Square. She was forty-six. Then the final victim, Mary Kelly, was killed, unlike the others, in her home in Miller's Court, Dorset Street, on Friday, 9 November. At the age of only twenty-five she was the youngest of the women to die.

The entry went on to list some of the suspects for the crimes. I did not know the names, though some of them seemed surprising to me – a member of the royal family, for instance – and then highlighted some of the details from the inquests and the killings themselves that might be clues for the identity of the Ripper. The ones that caught my attention were those that suggested the killer might have had medical knowledge. Some of the phrases from the inquests were quoted, and I scribbled all these details down in my notebook:

Those injuries, again, have in each case been performed with anatomical knowledge.

My own impression is that that anatomical knowledge was only less displayed or indicated in consequence of haste. The person evidently was hindered from making a more complete dissection in consequence of the haste.

There had been the same skill exhibited in the way in which the victim had been entrapped, and the injuries inflicted, so as to cause instant death and prevent blood from soiling the operator.

He must have had a good deal of knowledge as to the position of the abdominal organs, and the way to remove them.

The autopsies of the dead women established that in each case death was almost instantaneous; and that the ghastly mutilations were carried out after death. So it was clear to me that the killings were carried out by someone with medical knowledge and the skill needed to employ that knowledge at speed, in near darkness, with the ever-present threat of discovery. He was therefore likely to be arrogant about his abilities.

I looked across the reading room at my great-great-uncle's statue. What I was imagining now could not possibly be true. I thought of what Nanny had told Wyn, about Uncle Jack, and I knew that I had to look closely at the life of John Williams and prove to myself that I had got the wrong man, that I was on the wrong track. I hoped this would be the case.

Feverishly I started searching through Sir John's effects. At least, as feverishly as the National Library of Wales allowed me to. To order up an item you wish to see, you fill in a slip and hand this over to the reading room attendant, who disappears and returns a little while later with the book, or box, or whatever it is you have asked to look at. One at a time. The catalogue of his effects stated that, when Sir John passed his materials on to the library, and so to posterity, he left notes that I found in themselves revealing. Very carefully he recorded all the objects – with a few important exceptions – that he thought worthwhile keeping, and where they were placed in the drawers and cupboards of his home. His medals, for instance, some of them presented to him personally by Queen Victoria, were listed and stored 'in the top left-hand drawer of the desk in my study'. It is not just that he was doing what any well-ordered person would do: that is, tidy up the loose ends of his life before he dies and makes the job of an executor an easier one; it is a very clear statement on how he wanted the future generations to view him. I suppose we all feel this way, to a greater or lesser extent. I just can't see why he had taken the time and trouble to keep some of the things that he did, things which I think were very important to him – why else would he hold on to them through three household moves? – and yet not make any attempt to identify them for those he had asked to sort out his affairs after his death. I thought I would begin with these objects in case they led me to something unexpected.

While I waited in the small room, I looked around me. Under the watchful eye of the CCTV camera, there were four long tables, with chairs either side, so that about twenty or so people could read and work at the same time. When I first arrived, it seemed to be crammed with people working on their family histories, just like me. Someone had even come from Holland to look into his family's past. They all worked silently, so all you could hear was the clicking of laptop keyboards, the scratching of pencils, and the turning of ancient pages, crackling as they were fingered by the eager amateur detectives. Just like me, I thought again. Meanwhile, the library assistants busily whisked in and out of the inner sanctum where we mere readers were forbidden to tread, bearing weighty objects that were plonked down in front of the grateful recipients. Soon it was my turn; and, looking at the state of the box placed before me, I felt I was likely to be the first person to touch this box since it had been shelved.

Careful to appear as casual as possible, denying the trepidation I felt inside me, I knew that I must take care to show interest in papers other than those dated 1888 or later; that all of Sir John's life must become part of my thesis. So I reached for the box, and pulled it towards me. The first thing I pulled out was a knife, an ordinary knife – nothing special about it. What was this doing here? It was not a particularly nice knife, the sort of thing you would have been presented with, or a ceremonial one. It was obviously well used – the point had snapped off. Next were three glass slides, prepared for someone to look at under a microscope. Why were these in this box, and not in a laboratory or a museum somewhere? There was no indication either on the slides, or in the box with them, as to what was on the slides. I stared at them for a while, before returning them to the box to

14

continue looking through each item. A mat, a picture frame, an old cloak with a red lining, a binocular case, nothing that would tell me much.

I knew from looking at the lists of his belongings that not everything was here; there were too few boxes to contain all his collection. But no matter; I could study what I had, and piece together the story from the gaps and omissions as much as from what was there in my hands. His 1888 diary, for instance, from where the pages had been removed, although the thick blotting pages between them remained. The amount of ink on these pages showed that the diary had been extensively used. But why would you keep all your other diaries intact, and spoil only this one? For one reason only; you wanted to keep the events of that year secret. But then, why not destroy the whole book? Why keep the diary at all? To prevent anyone looking at the shelves and not seeing a diary for 1888, of course; to ensure that the semblance of normality was maintained.

I pressed on with my search. The next item, a medical note-book, in my great-great-uncle's handwriting, with lists of operations and names and dates alongside them –

Fistula   *Anne Deans*   *1882*

– that kind of thing. It was clear that he had kept a record of his own patients, something that referred to the ledgers in which their details were recorded in whichever hospital he had seen them.

Then came the moment that stopped me in my tracks. If there was a moment that chilled me, it was when I read this entry:

Abortion   Mary Ann Nichols   *1885*

I knew that name. She was killed, in east London, in 1888. The year Uncle Jack wrote to his brother to tell him he was unable to see him that night, that he was going to be attending a clinic in Whitechapel. I looked at my notes; the date on the letter, the date of the meeting, is 8 September. The second victim of the killings in Whitechapel was killed that night. Her name was Annie Chapman. Mary Ann Nichols, on whom my Uncle Jack had performed an abortion, was the first victim of the killer.

In his archive at the National Library of Wales, Sir John Williams left behind some of his notebooks. This volume was divided up by the condition suffered by each patient; the numbers after each name and date refer to papers presumably held in official records at the institutions where he treated these patients. This entry shows the name of the first victim of Jack the Ripper under the heading 'abortion'; the doctor has mistakenly slipped an extra 'e' into her name.

And now – in this windowless, neon-lit room, hundreds of miles from London and over a hundred and fourteen years since the murders happened – I began to believe I had discovered a terrible truth. I did not know what to do – should I tell someone, tell my family? Who would want to admit to being related to the most notorious British criminal ever? Would you? I know I did not.

Chapter Two

The feeling that I had discovered something that I was not meant to lingered with me for the next few days. It made it harder to have a normal conversation with my family; at first, I did not want to tell even my wife, Cathy, what I had learned. But eventually the information I had bottled up inside me had to come out. Not only did I need to tell her what I had found, I also needed to have someone question it. If she was convinced by my argument, then perhaps I would be convinced as well.

Or perhaps I wanted to poke holes in my findings; perhaps I wanted to be proved wrong. If so, I was wasting my time. Cathy was shocked at first, but then became as carried away by the story as I had been. Neither of us knew much about the Jack the Ripper killings but we made it our business to find out. We read an array of paperbacks from our local library; and nothing we read contradicted what little I knew about my great-great-uncle. But we also came up against a new problem; we now knew a lot about the Ripper, but comparatively very little about my relative.

I thought about what I knew from Wyn, and what Nanny had told him about the woman Uncle Jack had supposedly had an affair with. I thought that, if John Williams had some kind of secret life, my first step must be to uncover something about it, and maybe that would shed more light on whether or not my suspicions had any foundation. I needed to find out exactly who this woman was, and whether or not there could be any link to my relative. But how to go about this? Although I had spent time researching subjects before, those were fairly easy tasks; the books were in the library, nobody had anything to hide, it was all reasonably straightforward to put together. This was going to be very different; I would have to work hard to find the information I needed, and nowhere would this be more true than within my own family.

My mother and father had split up when I was about eight. After that I had had very little to do with my father for some years, though I had always known about his great passion for the Welsh nation and its cultural and historical inheritance, in particular the work of Dylan Thomas. I was sure he would know a great deal about the official side of John Williams's life. My dad was more interested in his literary and historical heritage – but was this what I wanted, though? It was the man's private and personal life which interested me, and to get that side of the story I would have to go to my mam.

From what Mam told me, she had spent a lot of her married life talking to Margaret, my father's mother, because Mam always found her mother-in-law to be what she called a 'straight-speaking person'. I suppose this was not surprising; living as she did only with men, my grandmother must have welcomed a woman to talk to, and to have her help around the house. My mother said to me once that she felt the old lady got on better with her and her children than she did with her own son, but of course I knew that she might say this to me simply because of the unpleasant atmosphere between my parents and their divorce.

I asked Mam about life when she married my father, and – without letting her know why – as much as I dared about my nan and her memories of John Williams. I knew that as Nan lived with her father and brother, the family's past was likely to have been a regular topic of conversation, especially when that past included a figure as illustrious as John Williams. And wouldn't a new member of that family, my mother, want to know all about the family she was joining? And, unlike my dad, I thought, she would want to know what kind of a man he was, what sort of family he had, what they thought of him, and what secrets had been kept hidden.

The first thing she told me was that Nan had spoken about the two branches of the family, physically separated by the Black Mountains, and how that had come about. 'Nanny said that the split came from a disputed will. Morgan Williams, who died in the first half of the nineteenth century, left the farm to his younger son David, and only one pound to his older son William.'

I almost laughed, it was such a mean thing to do. 'What was that about?'

'Nanny couldn't remember. It was so long ago, although she did say that the grudge went on for ages after. William lived until the 1870s so Nanny's own grandfather heard about the grudge at first hand. That's why one side of the family carried on living north of the mountain, in the old farm, and Nanny's side on the south, in a new farm William built. It was Nanny's grandfather who walked over the mountains to meet his cousins. So the bad feeling didn't last forever.'

I asked her about those cousins, and in particular John Williams. I had not told her before now about my trip to the National Library but she was not surprised to hear about my visit. I told her that my impression was of a successful, if withdrawn, man, and I asked her if Nanny had been proud of him and his achievements. And she told me much more than I expected, much more than I had hoped for.

'Yeah,' my mother replied, 'she was very proud of him. She said he had a surgery in Swansea and that he travelled back and forth to London.' After a moment, she continued, 'When she was a young girl there were whisperings about him carrying on with a girl called Mary, so they weren't very pleased with him at the time.'

I flinched at the sound of that name, but fortunately she did not notice. She did not know what I knew; that John Williams had written down Mary Ann Nichols's name in his notebooks – could it possibly be her? And that the last victim of the Ripper,

Mary Kelly, shared that name. Was it possible that Uncle Jack had had a relationship with one of them?

'Why did Nanny tell you this?'

'Oh, she was just talking about all her cousins and who she was belonging to, 'cause she often took me up to her cousin Ruby, and she was always talking about who belonged to her, distant relations and everything like that.'

Even though I knew some of this from Wyn, and from what I had pieced together already myself, it was still remarkable. Here was a name connected to the Ripper from someone who was not too young to have misheard it or to confuse it with something else. I began to feel that my suspicions were justified.

I looked up 'Mary' in one of the books about Jack the Ripper. I realised almost immediately that my first assumption was not likely to be correct; Mary Ann Nichols had lived most of her life in London. It seemed to me clear that Mary Kelly was more likely to have been the woman in question. She had been born in Ireland, but her family had moved to Wales when she was a young girl; she had gone on to live in Cardiff – not far from where I was now – and then moved to London. In London, she had worked as a prostitute and had travelled to Paris with one of her clients. She had been unhappy there, though, and after only a short time she returned to England. Once in London she went off the rails, and then fetched up dead in a Whitechapel hovel.

This set my pulse racing. She was in Wales, where my great-great-uncle was from. She travelled to London, where he lived and worked, and went to Paris with a 'gentleman'. My relative's marriage was rocked by a girl called Mary. Mary Kelly ended up in Whitechapel; John Williams wrote that he ran a clinic there.

There was nothing in any of this, I tried to tell myself; nobody would believe any of it. A policeman would not arrest someone on the basis of this kind of conjecture. And yet I was unable to get the idea out of my head. I continued to travel up to Aberystwyth, and work through the archive there. Following his footsteps at the library was an odd feeling for me; people at the library were always charming and helpful towards someone who they knew was related to the founder of the institution in which they worked. I was putting together a clear picture of Uncle Jack's life from the materials I read, and began to draft it into a kind of timeline so that I could start to make sense of what I had uncovered so far. I knew I might sometimes appear unfriendly to them, but as my researches progressed, I started to piece together the identity of the man that would shatter their views of him.

Chapter Three

I soon realised that I was going to need some help with this research. It was all very well driving up to the National Library in Aberystwyth, and visiting local relatives, but it was clear that I would need to uncover things in London, too, and that was going to need more time than I could manage. There would be police papers to read – and newspaper reports to track down – and who knew what else? From the contacts in publishing that I had made when my first book, *Island of Dreams*, came out, I spoke to one or two people without letting on what I was really looking into. I made contact with a researcher, Humphrey Price, who agreed to help me find out about the past of my family in Victorian London. At least, that is what I told everyone I was working on when I asked for their help, until I spoke to Humphrey on the phone.

It was not hard to find out that Humphrey had an interest in Jack the Ripper, and, once I had made certain that he would not pass on my story to anyone else, I told him what I knew about John Williams. At first, he did not really believe me, but when we met and I showed him some of the papers I had already copied, and we talked through what I had uncovered so far, he became as intrigued as I was. Humphrey told me that he had been interested in the Ripper story ever since seeing a programme on the TV about him as a boy, and had read all the principal books on the subject that had been published since then. He told me later that he had not expected much from our meeting, and that he had thought I would be some kind of trainspotter, my case based on arcane details such as pointing out why so-and-so's theory could not be the case as the timing showed a discrepancy of five minutes. In fact he was surprised that I did not know more about the earlier theories, but then realised why; I did not need to, as I had real evidence about my relative, and that was enough for me.

I told him about the small farm in Wales where John Williams was born, and about how his father had died when the boy was two, leaving him to be brought up alongside his three brothers by their mother. I showed him photographs of the doctor and his wife, and we looked at a map to see where Williams had lived in London, and how close this was to the murder sites. I told him about Mary Kelly's connections with Wales and about the 'Mary' of family legend; about the pioneering work in abdominal obstetric operations that my great-great-uncle performed; and about his work at University College Hospital, where he was during the autumn and winter of 1888. We looked at the papers I had copied, with Mary Ann Nichols's name alongside the description of the supposed killer by the only credible witness, George Hutchinson, that matched in many respects the description of the doctor given by John Williams's great friend, Herbert Spencer. We noted that John Williams, at the height of his profession in 1888, quietly left each official position and public medicine altogether within five years of the killings. We discussed his connection to the royal family. The diary, the knife, the slides, all came under consideration. We got on to the subject of a motive, and what John Williams's mental state might have been at the time of the murders. Humphrey asked me about the letters that were supposed to have been written by the Ripper to the police at the time; we looked at notes I had made from several accounts that dismissed most of the letters as fakes.

I had another letter to show him, a letter that I assumed John had written to Annie Roberts, a second cousin of his that he was supposed to marry. She went off and married someone else when he was away in London, studying. I had found it among others sent to her in his archive in the National Library; they must have been returned to John Williams at some point before he died. In this particular letter, the writing was cramped and messy, not the tidy print that he had used to enter Mary Ann Nichols's name in his register.

'It's impossible to read,' Humphrey said. 'I can't make any sense of it.'

'It's in Welsh, that's why. It's garbled as well. It's hard to make out anything even if you can read Welsh.' I showed it to someone, a Welsh speaker, who did not know who it was from and he said it was the work of a mad person. It says something like this:

There is shame on me sending a letter so small in a pouch so big to you. You are the seed/magic/illusion something something day. You are the centre of my world. I was thinking something something home and so sending a card to you and not the family. Thank you for the forgiveness and for keeping my secret. The analogy delay something something working something something physiological action: stimulating. It is bad of me unable to see you, but it's his dry insults. I had 13 out of 15 days troublesome ulcer something something the sunshine it would have troubled me more. At least ordination something something Tuesday when thinking of calling on you something something for a day or two, but I was feeling really terrible. Like the time I came ahead humming. Sit patiently and remember to wait for me.

See you

I finished reading from the letter. 'I've been wondering what he means,' I said, 'when he writes about 'keeping my secret'. Does he mean that the two of them had a secret that they didn't share with her husband – or was it more than that? And do you see the date on the envelope? Early 1889? Either way, it's not really the letter you'd write if you were thinking clearly, is it?'

We agreed to work together on this book. Before we did anything else, though, I asked Humphrey to agree on one important point. Nobody should know what we were really researching. We would not lie to them; investigating the background of an eminent Victorian surgeon, obstetrician and book collector would be reason enough to be doing what we were doing. We both knew, however, that until we could say for sure that we *knew* he was Jack the Ripper, it would be a mistake to say anything. Nobody would want to have any connection between their institution and those terrible crimes; and no one would want themselves or their family to be linked in any way to such a notorious killer. So we agreed that we would mention John Williams's name as our key point of our research, but certainly not mention exactly what it was about his life that we were researching. Until we were certain that we could publicly name John Williams as the Ripper, it would be wrong to allege anything against the man's memory. And we also knew that we would have to show some evidence to people, in order to back up our claims. If we could not, then the story would have to remain secret forever.

I had prepared myself to make a presentation to a sceptic and noted that, as I showed document after document to Humphrey, he became more and more convinced of my case. His interest in, and knowledge of, the subject meant that we were able to divide between ourselves the work we needed to do to provide the answer to various questions such as: what could have been in the missing diary pages? And what about the other things I had found in the library's archives? What could they mean? What happened to him in 1888? Where was his clinic? Why did he kill these women? What happened to him afterwards? Did anyone around him suspect anything? What about his wife? Did she know more about him than his affair? What was their relationship like? What was his life like?

Chapter Four

The *Lancet*'s obituary of John Williams, published in 1926, includes the line, 'In 1903, while still in the midst of successful practice, he retired to ... Llanstephan.'

The editors of the *Lancet* were not alone in noticing that John Williams retired early; the magazine of University College Hospital, in its obituary of him by his assistant, Dr Herbert Spencer, recorded that 'his comparatively early retirement from hospital practice [in 1893 was] due in part to his extensive private practice and in part to considerations of health'.

And yet not only did this 'unhealthy' man live on for another thirty-three years after he left UCH, twenty-three years after leaving London, but he also turned his back on part of his 'successful' private practice at that earlier date. Dr John Williams suffered some kind of breakdown, either at the end of the 1880s or at the start of the 1890s, that forced him to draw back from many aspects of his work, in the areas in which he operated, both public and private.

John Williams was born on 6 November 1840, in Beili, Gwynfe, his mother's family home, before being carried back to his family's farm, Blaen Llynant, in Llangadog in Carmarthenshire in rural Wales. His mother, Elinor, already had two sons, David and Morgan; she subsequently had a fourth, Nathaniel. Her only daughter, Elizabeth, died aged two and a half, barely three months after John was born. John's younger brother, Nathaniel, was the last of the line, as his father, David, died of typhoid fever when John was only two. John's birth was registered nearly a month after his birth, on 5 December, indicating that he was a healthy enough child (sick children in those days were quickly christened in case they died before being baptised into the Church). He certainly appeared healthy during his long life, living as he did until 1926, when he was aged eighty-six.

The farm nestled on a hillside by the north-west of the Brecon Beacons, hidden from the valley below, and, at the time John Williams was there, consisted of a solidly built farmhouse, where the family, their servants and farmhands, together with the local schoolmaster, lived; and a variety of outbuildings. Nowadays those outbuildings are cottages available for rent; the Big Barn is large enough to 'accommodate [a] string quartet for dinner'. Years ago, before the farm buildings had been converted, the yard would have looked very different from the smart and peaceful scene it is now. The day-to-day activity of the place, and the mess that would have gone with it all, have been replaced by a sloping lawn, tranquillity and ordered beauty.

John Williams's early life would have been part of this living farm and the rural activities that went with it. The farm had been managed by the family with the aid of a couple of farm hands, so it would have been a busy place, demanding of the time the residents of the farm could spare. Even the young John Williams would have found plenty of work for himself, with chores to be done both before and after school.

Elinor appeared to expect the very best from her sons and servants. The boys were taught to believe in a strict God, and this belief was rigidly enforced. Perhaps she felt she had to make up for the loss of their father. Not only did she teach her children to read and write in both Welsh and English, the servants were taught too – something that her neighbours regarded with suspicion, as an affectation of a woman trying to rise above her circumstances.

It must be remembered that in those days women were not yet allowed to own property. The Married Women's Property Act had not yet come into force, and it was only when it did, in 1870, that the laws regarding ownership of the home allowed married women to be on equal terms with men. So the suspicions of her neighbours might also have been heightened by their sense that she was herself slightly over-reaching her station in running a farm in the first place. Especially so when it turned out that she could run the farm better than many of the men who lived nearby, and that her farm became something of a model one in the area.

The best sources of information about John Williams's early life are two books: one written in Welsh about their mother, by John's younger brother Nathaniel; the other, written by Ruth Evans about John Williams himself, and published in both Welsh and English by the University of Wales Press at the behest of the National Library. Nathaniel's book was printed after her death – apparently paid for by John Williams – and runs to about ninety pages. It is a small book, with less than 170 words on every page. The frontispiece carries a photograph of Mrs Elinor Williams – a forbidding-looking woman, stern and unyielding in her gaze.

The fact that John lived a life so far removed from the rural farm of his childhood, with his houses in London, and his work for the royal family, shows that while Elinor was able to provide her sons with tremendous self-confidence, she was not able to encourage more than one of them to follow in her footsteps. It is interesting that John and his older brother fled the maternal nest when they could; John to London, and Morgan as far as the United States in order to do so. David, the eldest, stayed to work on the farm but he died when John was twenty-two, and it was left to the younger son, Nathaniel, tied to her apron strings, to work alongside his mother. Nathaniel stayed on the farm until he died in 1908, eighteen years before his older brother John, at the age of only sixty-five.

The real detail of John's childhood comes from a speech he made, when he was sixty years old, to the new intake of medical students at the University College of South Wales and Monmouthshire. In it he suggests much about his daily life as a small boy, although he does so in a roundabout way, referring to himself in the third person. We know from this speech, and from the few other sources left to us, that he was lively, outgoing and resourceful as a boy; but there is no hint in the boy's life of what was to come. We know that he was very fit, for he frequently refers to this in later life, certain that his health in his middle and old age stemmed from the daily exercise he had taken as a boy. We know he did not consider a career as a doctor until he was quite a lot older, and he appears to have been quite happy to have accepted the future his mother had devised for him as a minister. We know that on more than one occasion he addressed the congregation at the local chapel, where his father, David, had been Minister.

In the absence of her husband, Elinor Williams was a woman of high standards and high expectations. She 'was one of those rare women whose courage and faith never failed her and who, even when faced with sorrow and disaster, always found salvation in hard work,' said Ruth Evans. It sounds as if she were much like her more famous son; easy to admire for some, difficult to love for everyone. Nathaniel's book records her working tirelessly in the farm during the day and then sitting up into the night, reading voraciously. Sadly, we do not know what it was that she read so enthusiastically, but we can be sure it was of a religious bent. She lent horses, carts, farm hands and her own eldest son to help build the new Capel Maen Congregational Chapel in 1852, and then moved her family there to worship, abandoning the Reverend D. Jones's chapel of Bethlehem. It was in this chapel that her son John first preached.

John Williams was probably no different from most boys. He walked to school, as we know, for he tells us so often; the walk to the local school was three miles each way, and John Williams treasured this time not only for the love of healthy exercise it bred in him but also for the opportunity it gave him to explore the natural world. 'I confess that I look back upon this period of my life not only as one of the pleasantest and brightest but also as one of the best spent, for the effects have been my mainstay during the rest of my career,' he told the medical students of Monmouthshire in 1900. He continued:

Children had to walk to school from one to three miles in the morning and home again in the evening, carrying with them their midday meal. To accomplish this distance a boy took from an hour and a half to two hours in the morning. He reached the schoolroom at 9 o'clock and was supposed to work until 12 o'clock. Then followed a relaxation from work lasting two hours, a few minutes of which was occupied in partaking of a very simple meal, but a meal which was consumed with a relish and an enjoyment which many a luxurious epicure would give all but his dinner to possess. This meal, frugal as it was, was ample for the child's requirements. Then came the great pleasure of the day, hockey, football, or hare and hounds (cricket was unknown in country schools in those days), than which no exercises, games or gymnastics are better calculated. Thoroughly refreshed and untouched by fatigue the boy entered school again at 2 o'clock and remained until 4 o'clock. Then came the journey home, which occupied in winter at least two or three hours and in summer from three to four, with all its delightful incidents, unbeclouded by the thought of a home task [homework] – a new imposition condemned by every healthyminded boy. The boy never took the straight path or the shortest route. His curiosity, his inclination, his spontaneous energy, call it what you will, led him to deviate to the right and to the left from the normal course. He, moreover, required amusement and play after his exhausting labours in the schoolroom. There were various objects of interest which had to be visited on the way home. In a pool a mile up the stream on the left was the old trout, which had to be tickled or presented with various cunningly-devised invitations to land, to which his wariness never condescended to reply. On the right was the track of a hare. This had to be carefully inspected, while the discovery of a gin was a source of intense enjoyment and the division of its string afforded a doubly exquisite pleasure, for it ensured puss a free run and baulked the cunning and skilful poacher in his nefarious designs. Then the nest of an old crow upon a high and solitary tree should not be forgotten. It was some distance off, it is true, but it demanded a daily visit in the spring of the year, and the strongest and bravest boys climbed up in turn to inspect and count the eggs and in the end generally to rob the nest. This would sometimes lead to a falling-out – an event which is said to happen not rarely among thieves, but in this instance the honest bird did not come by its own. The encounter took some time to come to an issue. Unfortunately the morning told the story of the evening and this led to the application of the appropriate but unpleasant remedy.

Parts of the idyllic portrait of his youth reveal something of the man in the boy. Ruth Evans, who after all is kindly disposed to the subject of her book, writes that, as the leader of his little pack of friends, John Williams would assume lordly command over his fellows, and 'with sly persuasion' would get them not only to carry his satchel and books back for him, but 'sometimes even himself on their backs, when walking became a trifle irksome'. This ability of his to take charge of his peers, coupled with his assumption of superiority becomes increasingly familiar.

In later life, John Williams mentioned that he felt himself mentally stimulated by these walks home as well as physically stimulated, and he urged his students to do the same. 'All boys should be trained to use their eyes, their ears, and their hands ... Every lad should be taught early to use his eyes, to see and recognise the various objects, living and dead, which nature so bountifully supplies in earth, air and water.' Perhaps it was this early interest in the outside world that intrigued him, or – more likely – it was the benign influence of one of his teachers, for soon after, around 1855, he transferred from the local school in the Ceidrych valley to the Normal School in Swansea. His friends there, who went with him from Gwynfe, included Esay Owen, who was to marry Annie Roberts, the girl in the nearby farm to the Williamses.

Annie Roberts, always close to John Williams as a child, was also related to him, according to Ruth Evans. The farm, which was in the same area as the Williams farm in Gwynfe, was called Glantowy, and covered over 160 acres. Annie is called his 'second cousin' in some of the material that refers to her, but we have not been able to establish more about this family connection. The family tree he compiled showed no 'Annie Roberts', so perhaps this familial link was merely supposition, rather than an accurate record. But the census records did tell us that, at about the time that John Williams was walking the lanes to his school, Annie was living in the farm along with her father, mother, older sister, two servants and four farm workers, so their farm was much larger than the one managed by Mrs Elinor Williams.

The school that John Williams travelled to in Swansea was originally meant for teachers, to prepare them for their careers. While at the school, the young man continued to preach at the local chapel. But it was the head of the Normal School, Dr Evan Davies, who encouraged his interest in the natural world and the sciences, and it was here that John Williams deviated from the path his mother intended for him.

Elinor Williams had wanted her son to take a career in the ministry, and everything in his life so far had been geared towards that. Apart from the influence of Dr Davies, though, it is hard to know what persuaded him to stand up to his formidable mother. One thing is sure, though; John Williams was brought up by his mother to think quite highly of himself. She gave him an enormous sense of his own self-worth; a confidence which enabled him to leave her and head for Scotland, and a year's study of mathematics at the university in Glasgow. Later in life John Williams acknowledged that neither he nor his mother knew what he was going to do after that, though he knew enough by then to know that his future did not lie in the chapels of Wales. 'Certain I am, however, that neither my mother, who was my guide, nor I myself had worked out any positive scheme or definite plan as to the future of my education, nor as to my business in life.'

John Williams must have enjoyed his time in Glasgow. He kept his lecture notes and all these years later they can still be read in the archives of the National Library of Wales. The first outside account of him came from his teacher, Professor Blackburn, who wrote a report on the year he spent there. It tells us that he attended classes with 'unfailing regularity', that in his exams he answered 'extremely well', his conduct in class was 'excellent', and his exercises 'admirable'. He won second prize for 'general excellence', as voted for by his classmates, and his professor thought this something to which he was 'fully entitled'.

What does all this tell us so far? John Williams was physically strong, naturally curious, determined, ambitious, used to assuming a position of preeminence among his peers, hardworking, successful academically if not outstanding at this point; in short, he possessed many of the characteristics that we would see later on in his working and private life.

After his year in Stanhope Street, John Williams returned to Wales and very quickly decided on his future. Perhaps something happened in Glasgow to clarify matters for him. There were no doctors in the immediate family, so it is hard to know where the impulse came from. Perhaps he was influenced by a family friend; perhaps something he had learnt at school aroused his curiosity. Clearly he wanted to do something other than go into the ministry; and when he returned home in July 1859 he took up the first post in his long medical career, as an apprentice to two Swansea general practitioners, Dr Ebenezer Davies, who had trained at Guy's Hospital in London, and Dr

W. Henry Michael, who had lately been the Officer for Health in Swansea. Maybe it was thanks to the enthusiasm of Dr Davies, or perhaps it was already in John Williams's mind, but after he had worked for two years as apprentice to the two doctors, he moved to London to continue his medical career there.

John Williams was a supremely confident man; although he came from a small Welsh valley, he and his brothers were encouraged by their mother to feel they could accomplish anything they set their minds to, and London cannot have seemed such an extraordinary choice for the young man. After all, his elder brother Morgan was already in the United States, where, in just a few years from then, he would join up with the Heavy Artillery Regiment of New York and fight on the Union side in the American Civil War. With that example in mind, London cannot have seemed so very far away to the twenty-one-year-old John Williams. Ambition was something that he shared with Morgan, but it seemed to have eluded their younger brother, Nathaniel, who was content to remain at his mother's side till she died.

In December 1861 John Williams started his formal training at University College Hospital in Gower Street in London, where he was a remarkably successful student. What was London like when John Williams arrived? The city then was not the extraordinary capital of the empire it later became at the height of Victoria's reign, when a doctor was a significant figure in society; it was still a city in transition. Refugees in their thousands from Eastern Europe were entering the capital. Although the Metropolitan underground railway had been opened, most transport was by horse, whether in a carriage or a horse-drawn omnibus. The sewage system had yet to be properly established – the vast underground constructions that still function as London's sewers, and which shifted the filth from the streets, were only completed by the end of the decade. But the visitor to London would have marvelled at the scale of everything around him – whether it was the size of the buildings or the numbers of people living among them. 'The visitor who finds himself for the first time on London Bridge is distracted by the rush of life, the noise of wheels, the trampling of horses, and the murmur of myriads of voices, and other confused sounds, that seem to fill the air,' wrote the *Cassell's Illustrated Guide to London* for 1862. The guide's writers feel impelled to tell us, with the kind of efficient Victorian bureaucracy that we were coming to know so well, that 107,000 people used the bridge every day, and that 20,000 vehicles crossed it as well. They go on: 'But the order that prevails in all this confusion is greater than the din of business, and soon makes itself felt. In a few moments, the most unsophisticated rustic will acquire perfect confidence, feeling that it is no turbulent crowd, but an ordered march of intelligent beings, of which he finds himself a part.'

We know enough about John Williams to know that he would not have considered himself an 'unsophisticated rustic', but nevertheless he would have been impressed by the view from London Bridge. Towering above the city was St Paul's Cathedral, but it was not alone on the skyline – many of today's sights were there as well. The monument to the Great Fire of London, Mansion House, Westminster Abbey, the Houses of Parliament, Lambeth Palace – all of these would have been sights for the young John Williams to see on his arrival in the capital.

As well as the churches no doubt prescribed by his mother, the young Welsh student would have visited the musical halls, the theatres, and other places of entertainment.

Perhaps he would have ventured a little further afield. The *Cassell's Guide* does not cover Whitechapel, but it leads the reader through the docks (so that it was possible to witness London's vibrant trade with the world) and only here mentions one of the downsides to London: the whores, or 'drabs', on the lookout for sailors ready to spend their wages. Here too, we are told, 'gin and beer in this region dispute the possession of our olefactories with tar'.

We can know a little more about the young student's life from reading the memoirs of other students. Shepherd T. Taylor wrote about his student days at King's College from the years 1860 to 1864, and experienced life in London much as John Williams did. He too was a boy from a rural background, only in his case it was Norfolk, and he too had benefited from some experience of medical practice before coming to study in London. He often visited the churches of London, twice a day on Sunday, so he was no less religious than John Williams; he even on a few occasions heard the Reverend W. W. Champneys, father of John Williams's friend Francis preaching in later years. He too visited the music halls, and the theatre ('1 October 1860. In the evening I commenced my career of dissipation by going to the Strand Theatre, where we had three or four very lively comedies, which pleased me'), and visited the notorious Haymarket, where 'there must have been at least a thousand ladies of easy virtue assembled there of all nationalities, some of whom were very anxious to do business with me'. He also described some of his botanical lectures, on 'Subdivisions of Cryptogamia and Phanerogamia', which he found very interesting. He was taught by Dr Partridge, who lives up to the image of the medical teacher in that he made coarse jokes throughout his lectures of such vulgarity that Shepherd Taylor was shocked. He also found dissection rather hard to take: 'A bonny buxom maiden with plenty of flesh on her bones is no doubt a pleasing spectacle for God and men to look on in the ball-room, but when her poor dead body is resting on a table in the dissecting room, it is a veritable horror to the student who is called upon to dissect it.' He also wrote about the days when dissections were impossible because of the thickness of the London fog that enveloped the room.

As Shepherd Taylor progressed towards his goal of qualifying as a doctor, he had to take on tasks outside his hospital, such as visiting women when they gave birth. 'Visited one of my future midwifery cases in Acorn Court, Chancery Lane, having to traverse a perfect maze of cut-throat passages to reach my destination. Doctors, however, are never molested or maltreated in these slummy districts.' John Williams was to find this out for himself years later.

It would have been fascinating to read John Williams's impression of his first few years in London; if only he had left a record such as Shepherd Taylor's. The young man from the Welsh valleys, naïve and inexperienced as he must have been, would have found all of London's varied entertainments fascinating, even if he started with the religious zeal necessary to ward off the more sinful of them. As to the hospitals, he would have been only too well aware that the general view of them, as displayed here from an article in *Punch* magazine of 1842, was not that high:

> The readiest way to arrive at any of these noble Institutions is to slip down under a loaded omnibus in a neighbouring thoroughfare, from which spot the journey is easy and pleasantly performed on a shutter, with a large train of attendants, who readily offer their services to escort you. These edifices have in view the provision of subjects for anatomy, the pecuniary benefit of their officers, and the trial of new remedies upon a class of mortals who, from their resigned tractability, are termed patients; whilst the wards form an agreeable promenade for a number of studious and scientific young men of the day.

We can also glimpse something of the working life of students and the environment in which they operated from the records of Dr Cuthbert Locker. Dr Locker wrote about his time, in 1887, when 'as a student, I remember that our senior surgeon at my Alma Mater [the Charing Cross Hospital] could be seen to enter a small room adjacent to the main entrance to the hospital and don a frock-coat with its sleeves stained with blood and grease from previous operations. With the said sleeves turned up, he would go into the operating theatre, wash his hands and proceed to do a major operation.' The patient was strapped on a table, and the students stood on semicircular rows of benches and watched the surgeon at work. In the days before anaesthetics, it would have been an appalling experience to witness. However, by the time John Williams was practising, anaesthetics were becoming commonplace. The use of ether to render a patient insensible from pain had started in America in the 1840s, although it had originally been suggested by the British chemist Humphrey Davy back in 1800. The popularity of chloroform in operations was boosted by Queen Victoria having it administered to her during childbirth, and it became regularly used by the doctors of the 1860s.

More importantly from our point of view, 'Listerism', named after its chief practitioner, Dr Joseph Lister, was making its appearance while John Williams was studying. This innovation involved the use of antiseptics to help prevent the spread of infection during and after an operation. Before this time, the most trivial operation was likely to be followed by infection, and death occurred in up to 50 per cent of all surgical cases. A review of hospitals published in 1894 stated that, during the late 1860s and throughout the 1870s, when John Williams was right in the midst of this time of change and progress, hospitals were 'places which healthy people should avoid and sick people should shun,' because of the risk of infection there. After Louis Pasteur discovered that bacteria caused fermentation, Lister realized in 1865 that the formation of pus was also due to germs. At first, he used carbolic acid sprays to kill germs in the air, but later he realized that germs were also carried by the surgeon's hands and instruments. He insisted on the use of antiseptics on hands, instruments, dressings, and on the patient.

John Williams worked alongside Marcus Beck, Lister's nephew, and they became friends; Beck was to be John Williams's best man at his wedding in a few years' time. Later on in his career, Williams assiduously followed the use of these antiseptic practices within his chosen field, obstetrics, but to have practised them in his student days would have been nothing less than revolutionary. Some of his contemporaries still felt that boiled water and speed were the prerequisites of a successful operation. That many doctors resisted the use of antiseptics seems bizarre.

To his contemporaries, John Williams was therefore something of an innovator, recalled today for his 'pioneering work' in abdominal operations as an obstetrician.

John Williams had been trained by doctors who had themselves learned their trade in the mid nineteenth century, with the values and expectations of that age. So the way the medical profession developed during those decades is relevant in the sense that the principles John Williams adopted were learned in those classrooms and surgeries. He might well have learned from these men as much as from teachers such as Lister. In Ruth Richardson's book on the Anatomy Act, established after various cases of body-snatching in the early nineteenth century, she writes that:

> Throughout the nineteenth century, the surgical and administrative elites of Britain were prepared to turn a blind eye to (sometimes gross) breaches of decency and of the Act's regulations, so long as the public was kept in ignorance and the dissecting tables supplied. The profession itself had long roots in illegality and negligence towards popular feeling, and as a profession went along with the letter of the Act only so far as it suited itself to do so. The only Victorian change to the Act was made in 1871, and was the result of persistent non-compliance of anatomists with the burial clause. It simply permitted a longer period in which to dissect.

Poor people feared the hospitals in those days; they knew that they would be hacked about by men in frock-coats, and that they were supposed to be grateful for it. The famous surgeon Frederick Treves who had brought Joseph Merrick, the Elephant Man, into the hospital where he eventually died, noted in his autobiography, published some thirty-five years after the Ripper killings:

> The hospital in the days of which I speak [the mid-to-late 1870s] was anathema. The poor people hated it. They looked upon it primarily as a place where people died. It was a matter of difficulty to induce a patient to enter the wards. They feared an operation, and with good cause, for an operation then was a dubious matter. There were stories afloat of things that happened in the hospital, and it could not be gainsaid that certain of these stories were true.

Doctors were 'heroes', taking on the limits of society's approval for a new technique, and ensuring it was adopted. 'Heroic efforts' are the words the doctors applied to treatment that cost lives then, but ultimately contributed to the greater good. What words can be given to treatments that were perceived as 'heroic' by the doctor carrying them out, yet which never saved a single life? Who is to say that the first people killed by Jack the Ripper died on the streets of Whitechapel, and not on an operating table? Who is to say that John Williams was not 'pioneering' an operation that he thought might alleviate a condition within women – that is, infertility? And that he tried to enlarge his knowledge of infertility in order to treat sufferers such as his wife by experimenting on poor women from the East End? There is no evidence of this; but then no one would keep records of poor women who had died with no discernible benefit to anyone else.

Little is known about John Williams's time in London when he was a student. University College Hospital was his main base, but records of where he lived while he worked at the hospital are nowhere to be found. He studied the following: anatomy (with dissections); physiology (including general physiology and morbid anatomy); chemistry; practical chemistry; *Materia Medica* (essentially, the branch of medicine to do with preparing and using drugs); botany; forensic medicine; theory and practice of medicine; theory and practice of surgery; midwifery; and hospital practice. He was a conscientious and hard-working student, and when he finally became a doctor he carried with him medals and certificates to show that he had been one of the best candidates of his year. He was awarded many prizes: in 1862, a silver medal for chemistry; in 1863, one for anatomy and physiology; and, chief among these, in 1864, a gold medal for pathological anatomy. The medal was made of gold, and, when he married a few years later, he punched out some of the gold to melt into a ring for his wife which he fashioned himself.

Also in 1864, when he was made assistant to the Obstetric Physician at UCH, he began working in the area of medicine that was to consume all his later life. He achieved his first medical qualification, Licentiate of the Apothecaries' Society (LSA) in 1865; this enabled him to take up a post as house surgeon in University College. He moved to Brompton Hospital and then to Great Ormond Street Hospital for Sick Children, during which time he qualified as a member of the Royal College of Surgeons (1866) and became a Bachelor of Medicine. In the following year, he finally achieved his aim of becoming Doctor of Medicine. Given that he returned there, he must have enjoyed living in London, and certainly he knew that if he were to fulfil his ambitions, it would be in London hospitals. It is unlikely that his mother felt the same; doubtless she had brought him up to speak both English and Welsh because she wanted her son to contribute to the life and culture of Wales. Through the library, he more than fulfilled her aim, but everything indicates that she would have liked him to return to

Wales as soon as he had completed his studies in London and to set up in practice in Wales.

At this point, things stopped going his way for the boy from rural Wales. Instead of staying on the path recommended for aspiring young doctors – that is, to take a job at a hospital in London and learn his profession there – he returned to Swansea to become a general practitioner. Perhaps John Williams felt he owed his mother a duty of care for the sacrifices she had made so that he could travel to Glasgow and London to study? Living and studying in London cannot have been cheap, especially when compared to rural Wales; his board and lodging had come part and parcel with University College Hospital, but his mother had paid for her son's other expenses, as well as the cost of tuition, amounting to what would have been between £73 and £105 a year, with books, instruments, examination and registration fees on top.

Or was this his first professional setback? Despite his outstanding career as a student, John Williams failed to be taken on at any of the London hospitals where he had trained, and he returned to Swansea to seek work not within a large teaching hospital but as a general practitioner. Perhaps he regretted his choice of specialisation, although it would have been possible to further his interest in obstetric medicine – defined as 'medical care in pregnancy and childbirth' – within the confines of his practice.

So either Williams turned his back on London or it turned its back on him. John Williams would have to live in Swansea, and work there for some years, before he would be welcomed back.

While John Williams had been away in London, his old employer in Swansea, Dr W. Henry Michael, had retired. Dr Michael's position had been taken instead by Dr Davies – the practice was now known as Davies and Davies. Dr Andrew Davies had previously been a surgeon in the coalmines of Wales, working for the Golynos and Varteg Iron and Coal Works. Dr Ebenezer Davies had taken up another role as well; he was also

Admiralty Surgeon and Agent. Shortly after John Williams returned from London, Davies and Davies moved, and Dr Ebenezer Davies changed jobs once again, this time becoming Medical Officer for Health in Swansea. John Williams returned and gradually took over the patients of his former employers; they moved on, with Dr Andrew Davies moving west from Swansea to become a surgeon at the Cardiff Infirmary, later known as the Cardiff Hospital. John Williams set up his practice in 10 Heathfield Street. He proudly displayed his credentials so that his new patients would know that this was not the apprentice of former days, but a fully-fledged London doctor who they were dealing with. If John Williams found it depressing to return to Wales, qualified for working in a major hospital and instead found himself treating patients out of a house in a small street in Swansea, there was also another huge disappointment awaiting him. The woman he had wanted to marry had married his best friend while he was away in London. Annie Roberts had chosen Esay Owen over John Williams, and this left him alone amidst the circle of friends he had made in Swansea earlier.

In the National Library of Wales archives, there are some photographs of Esay Owen and his wife with Lizzie, who married John Williams, showing a marked contrast between the two women. Mrs Williams is drawn, thin, ill–looking; Mrs Owen is bright and smiling, cheerful in the company of two men who love her. The letters we read showed that he had swallowed his pride and stayed in touch with them both for the rest of their lives. No wonder Lizzie looks out of sorts.

However, the Annie in the photographs was not the one that John Williams had hoped to marry, but a new Mrs Owen. These letters indicate that he also loved her. Once again, Lizzie must have felt overshadowed by another woman. During her life with John Williams, it seemed, there were many others.

On her wedding certificate, 6 January 1864, Annie Owen declares her age as twenty-one; however, in the 1881 census, which shows her living with 'Evan' Owen, her daughter Edith, and her sons John and Arnold, as well as a teacher, Mary Hughes, and their servant, Margaret Rees, shows that 'Sophia A. C. Owen' is forty-three years old – a difference of twenty-two years after a gap of only seventeen years. West Glamorgan Archives Centre solved the problem. Esay and Annie had a daughter, also confusingly named Annie; shortly after her daughter was born, Annie died of scarlet fever, on 29 November 1864, aged twenty-two.

Five years later, on 28 September 1869 Esay Owen, then thirty-four, remarried, a woman herself widowed, Sophia Ann Charlotte Evans, aged thirty-two. Sophia does not appear to have brought any children to the marriage; census reports list the daughter 'Annie' but then she was omitted from later ones. Had she left home? Did she, too, die? The coincidence of the name Annie explained the anomalies creeping into the documents about her, but it also indicated a couple of other things.

Firstly, John Williams must have become used to death not only as an occupational hazard but also as a personal issue, a grief to be overcome. His father had died young; Lizzie Hughes's mother had died young; and now we had learnt that the love of John Williams's youth had also died young. He seemed to be surrounded by death.

Secondly, we had assumed wrongly that the letter of early 1889, in which John Williams had shown signs of a mental collapse, was written by him to his former sweetheart, Annie. Now we knew differently; that far from being a hangover from his earlier life, the ardour and desire for secrecy stemmed from a romantic attachment outside his marriage with Sophia, also known as Annie.

Esay and his family lived in Clydach, and the school he helped to found is still there today. In the 1881 census, the independent minister is listed as living with his wife, Sophia Ann, their daughter, and their two sons John (possibly named after John Williams) and Arnold, and a servant. Esay Owen died on 26

June 1905, and was outlived by his second wife by some fifteen years.

But back in Swansea in the late 1860s, John Williams may have felt isolated by Annie's change of heart and his friend Esay's marriage to a woman he had regarded as special to him, and so while he would have spent time with new acquaintances discussing Welsh culture and walking the hills around Swansea, he would certainly have found time to see his former employer, Dr Ebenezer Davies and his new partner, Dr Andrew Davies. Perhaps John Williams would have asked them for help in establishing himself in practice in Swansea. In any event, in under a year he had moved to 13 Craddock Street and there he practised until 1872. While he worked there, he also took on other employments, perhaps learning from the Drs Davies; in the early 1870s he became the Medical Officer of the Post Office in Swansea (a job that Ebenezer took over after John left Swansea). Dr Andrew Davies, meanwhile, after some time as President of the Swansea and Monmouthshire Medical Association, a society that John Williams would have belonged to, left the partnership with Dr Ebenezer Davies, and retired to Cardiff.

John Williams quickly established himself within the professional world in Swansea. He joined societies, such as the local medical ones, and he also joined the Freemasons. The Freemasons have long had their name associated with the Jack the Ripper crimes, but there is nothing in John Williams's story to suggest that there is any involvement of any sort with the Freemasons in the deaths of the five women on the streets of Whitechapel. However, it cannot be denied that one of the advantages of joining the Freemasons for a young man such as John Williams would be the innumerable contacts it would provide him with. Although there is no evidence for this, one thing that might have kept John Williams above suspicion later was that he did have contacts at the highest levels within the police force and the upper echelons of London society.

Of course, you cannot just join the Freemasons, you must be invited, and it is likely that the man who invited John Williams to join him in the brotherhood was his future father-in-law, Richard Hughes.

Chapter Five

Where they met we do not know, but, after the heartbreak over Annie Roberts, John was to turn his attention to a younger woman, Lizzie Hughes. The daughter of an industrialist, she lived in Morriston, Swansea. Morriston at the time was a thriving area of development and the Hughes family were highly thought of.

Richard Hughes was a partner in the Landore Tin Plate Works, established in 1851, and based in Swansea. He was one of four co-owners; the Landore was a large plant, one of the biggest and, in its day, one of the most modern in Wales. Later on, the site would also be used for one of the most revolutionary processes in steel-making in the UK, but for the tin-plate manufacturers times were good for the first forty years or so of their business. The company grew to employ almost one thousand people and was regarded as one of the more forward-thinking parts of the industrialised belt in south Wales. When, in 1874, there was a massive strike throughout the region – caused by the employers locking out the workers who were seeking better rates of pay – it was the Landore workers who voted to return to work first, with the employers taking the opportunity to welcome them back by playing them into the pay office with a brass band. As they queued to collect their old rates of pay, the humiliation of the workers was complete.

In Lizzie Hughes, John Williams had chosen for himself a refined, talented, and religious girl. She played the organ in her local chapel and the congregation gave her a special present on her wedding day of a 'set of silver side dishes', together with a 'really beautiful Bible'. Quite what she expected from her husband is hard to know. Of course he needed her: a wife was 'almost a necessary part of a physician's professional equipment,' said H. B. Thompson in *The Choice of a Profession*, published in 1857; because women would not feel comfortable being attended by a bachelor doctor. John Williams also thought his wife more than a professional accoutrement and a social adornment; he believed that she would provide him with children.

Mary Elisabeth Ann Hughes was born in March 1850, only daughter of Richard Hughes (born 1829) and Ann Thomas (born 1830). Richard Hughes's first wife died young, and he then married Mary, some sixteen years his junior. Lizzie was obviously the apple of her father's eye, as we can see in the photos held in John Williams's archive at the National Library. An article about her marriage to John Williams, in April 1872, records that 'the bride herself' shows:

> a willingness with which she has on occasions come forward to aid by her efforts and influence all movements having for the object the moral and religious improvement of the people, ... and the unassuming kindness of her disposition has endeared her to all her neighbours, who have watched her course from childhood upwards ...

This makes her sound a little saintly, but it is likely that, as an only daughter (and the only child born to a deceased wife) the mine-owner's daughter from parochial Wales was spoiled by her father. Marriage would be very different. Her husband, indeed society in general, would have strong opinions about how an eminent doctor's wife, in the centre of Victorian professional aristocracy, should behave. Whatever else we can sense about their marriage, despite signs of a closeness between the two of them at least in the initial stages, it was certainly a match that centred around him. The same newspaper report that gushed over Lizzie Hughes also tells us that the service was short, conducted in Welsh, and that he – not her, unlike in other marriage services of the time – was asked some questions. Lizzie's place in the marriage – silent and obedient – was firmly established from the outset.

Her diary for that year is one of the few objects belonging to her in the archive of the National Library, but it is he, not her, who fills in the first few entries. He records details of their wedding (but no mention is given to his beloved mother), spending about as much time recounting the amusing story of how his best man Marcus Beck slept through his connection on the train as he does on the wedding itself. As an afterthought, he adds, 'Liz looked in travelling dress better than ever.'

Both man and wife write entries during their honeymoon. Ever the worker, he spent a portion of their time on the continent visiting hospitals – one, Lizzie noted, 'appears more like a huge workhouse than an hospital' (23 April). Perhaps it was while on his honeymoon that John Williams forged contacts with other obstetricians that later led to him being an honorary member of a number of obstetrical societies all over the world.

In early May they returned home. Around the time that John Williams proposed to Lizzie, the opportunity to work in London had presented itself again. Lizzie went back to Wales while her husband, together with her father, travelled to London to sort out a suitable home for their married life. Lizzie retired to bed, writing (on 6 May) that she was 'in bed most of the day. Great fun watching the rabbits.' This immaturity raises doubts as to how she would have coped with the formidable society ladies in London; the naive girl from the provinces would have been overawed by the more worldly women she encountered through her husband's circle at UCH.

In her diary she continued to refer to her husband as Dr Williams. It was not until 21 June that she called him 'John' – which was interesting given that she referred to a number of her other friends by their first names. We are also afforded a more private glimpse into their lives; Dr Williams sat up the evening of 15 July, 'till past 1 a.m.', reading George Eliot's novel *Romola*. In late July, they moved into 28 Harley Street, in the heart of London, and, shortly afterwards, 'John began doing Dr Hewitt's work.' That autumn there was a flurry of family activity involving many trips to Shrewsbury, which ended in mid-November when 'Annie Hughes left Shrewsbury'. The entry for 24 November reads: 'John and I so happy alone.'

One evening in late December 1871, a Welsh doctor called Fred Roberts was returning to London after performing an operation in Pembrokeshire. He stayed the night with a friend in Swansea, Dr Griffiths, and there he met one of Dr Griffiths's colleagues, Dr John Williams. They discussed a recent vacancy at University College Hospital, that of the position of Assistant Obstetric Physician. The position had not been filled and the two doctors urged John Williams to apply. Rather than write, John Williams travelled to London to apply for the post, but when he arrived the application period had closed and he was too late. However, the doctor saw the Dean, who decided that the young Welshman was an impressive candidate and so reopened the position, to which John Williams was successfully appointed. That which he had been after for some time – a return to the capital, and the chance to make his mark there – was back within his grasp.

Throughout John's career there was to be a question mark over the way that he was appointed to this position. On the surface, there was no impropriety, but this did not stop people considering it as somehow out of order. Even as late as 1891, an article appeared in which it was suggested that 'this was the beginning of the bitterness which has since dominated the intercourse between Dr Williams and a certain section of his colleagues'.

The questions this leaves begging are these: if he was so evidently the right candidate for the job – as shown by the Dean's decision to reopen the application process for him – why was he not considered before the advertisement was placed, or the process closed to applicants, by his former colleagues? Having worked in *exactly* that position only a few years previously, why was John Williams not considered straight away for the post? He clearly did not have a champion at UCH, someone who wanted to see him appointed to the job, and one must assume that the person who stood in his way was his immediate superior, the Obstetric Physician, Dr Graily Hewitt. And was he truly ignorant of the job before being urged to apply for it by his two friends? Had he decided to settle down in Swansea, until this opportunity was put in front of him? Something spurred his ambition – or had it just lain dormant for a while? Perhaps his marriage had reawakened it; perhaps his confidence had been dented by the move away from London, and it took the encouragement of friends to make him feel he was ready to move back there. Perhaps it was simply that he and his new bride wanted to experience life beyond Swansea, and the chance to do so arose at this most opportune of moments. What is certain is that his appointment provoked little admiration and a fair amount of envy.

Young doctors in those times did not expect this to be the way their careers began. In *The Medical Profession in Mid-Victorian London*, M. Jeanne Peterson writes:

In his last year of medical studies, a student was required to serve at least three months as a clinical clerk to a hospital physician or as a dresser to a surgeon. These posts involved the basic care of medical and surgical patients in the wards under the supervision of the house physicians and surgeons, who were in turn responsible to the senior staff.

Beyond the immediate educational value of these posts, they often had far-reaching career effects. Clerks or dressers serving under the same houseman became known as a "firm". They often kept close ties, either personal or professional, long after medical school. Such friends could be a source of patients or consulting work. Senior men recommended their dressers and clerks to ... a variety of other appointments that helped them start their careers.

If he had ambitions to rise to 'the top of the tree', it was important to stay in London, to continue his affiliation with the world of hospitals and medical teaching, and eventually to gain appointments at the centre of English medical life.

Qualifying at age twenty-one, the aspirant to consulting status stayed in London, serving in minor hospital posts, seeking the beginnings of practice, and making what connections and income he could. At age twenty-six, he became a Fellow of his college and, with luck, by age thirty he might be appointed assistant physician or surgeon at one of the London hospitals.

If this was a template for a young doctor's career, then John Williams did not follow it. At almost every point, the young Welsh doctor did the opposite. So John Williams's return to London was very much against the grain. It must have been an interesting time for him to return – and to be set up with a house in Harley Street – when he was not a favourite with his seniors in the hospital. No wonder, then, that his first few years in London were financially tough for him. Did this help to set him apart further? Did the envy aroused because of the apparent ease of his appointment manifest itself in his peers obstructing his career in private practice? Was he always to be an outsider? And being the outsider, did he feel that he had to work harder, to prove himself more, to discover something remarkable that no one else knew? To discover a cure or to refine a process that no one else had tried? A young doctor could make his name, his career, and his fortune this way. John Williams had been taught by one such man, Dr Joseph Lister. Was he inspired to do the same himself? After all, these were the times of innovation – of 'heroic' work by doctors. John Williams resolved to pioneer research on the uterus and the ovaries.

Chapter Six

Eager and ambitious, Dr Williams added to his workload under Dr Graily Hewitt by taking on the position of Medical Officer for Out-Patients at Queen Charlotte's Lying-In Hospital in Marylebone Road. With characteristic self-aggrandisement, he submitted his entry to the *Medical Directory* with the rather more pleasing title of Physician to the Out-Patients.

He had also become a member of the Obstetrical Society of England and Wales. This excellent body would meet regularly to discuss papers presented by members, to air issues relating to their jobs (for example, the unregulated midwives that they sought to control), to examine unusual cases and dissect the malformed babies and other parts of the body that fellows around the country had encountered during their work. Their unquestioned superiority in Victorian society was evident at one meeting when an eighteen-year-old girl with anomalies to the skin around her nipples was brought in and asked to display her breasts to the forty or so fellows of the Society gathered in the room. There was no suggestion of a chaperone for her. The meeting continued with presentations from the doctors of the 'monsters', the deformed babies and deformed wombs that were offered up for fellows to volunteer to dissect.

Early on in his relationship with the society – within two years of joining – John Williams was made Honorary Secretary, yet, as ever, all was not plain sailing for him. It is interesting to read the proceedings of their meetings. There were usually between forty to fifty fellows present, sometimes more, with one or two distinguished visitors (often doctors from abroad), as well as a handful of doctors applying for membership. Often the papers presented were extraordinarily long and discussion of the paper would have to be postponed to the following meeting – John Williams himself was known for writing lengthily. What is fascinating, though, is how contentious his papers seemed to be. The custom of the society was to thank the speaker for their paper before the floor was opened up for critical appreciation. In John Williams's case, fellows sometimes did not even bother with the polite remarks of thanks before launching into well-argued and reasoned attacks on his position on the issue of the moment. For example, after the Welsh doctor's presentation in May 1882 of a paper on 'The Natural History of Dysmenorrhoea', Dr Savage remarked that Dr Williams's paper was 'so long and elaborate that one forgot the beginning of it'. This treatment was not just meted out when he was a junior member of the society; even after he had been President in 1887, the other fellows were extraordinarily abrupt in their remarks.

From similar minutes in the college archives, we can see what John Williams's life at University College Hospital was like. He spent most of the 1870s consolidating his position there, and he expanded his repertoire by moving on from Queen Charlotte's and becoming a Consultant Physician at the Royal Infirmary for Women and Children at Waterloo. In 1880, he became Consultant Physician at the St Pancras and Northern Dispensary in the Euston Road. His private practice must have grown, too, though not always easily; it would have helped this aspect of his career when he was made a Fellow of the Royal College of Physicians in 1879, and perhaps this is what enabled him and Lizzie to travel to the West Indies in 1881.

John Williams has left us a diary of this trip, and it affords us a rare insight into the state of his marriage. His handwriting is difficult to decipher, almost impossible in the later pages. The writing starts off clean and fine but swiftly becomes crabbed and slanted. The transcripts supplied by the Library omit the more unreadable passages. But, as one of the few records that allows us to see something of their married life and how distant he seemed from her, it is invaluable. The diary has only survived in a partial form, so we do not get to read about everything they experienced on their trip. Nevertheless we can make out enough to get a sense of their voyage and what they experienced. They visited Jamaica and Barbados, and neither of them was a particularly good sailor. Once on dry land, John Williams seems to spend most of his time away from his wife, out riding in the hills with his new travelling companions. This extract from his diary gives a rare insight into their relationship.

Everything having been made ready, we started from Waterloo station by Royal Mail carriages to Southampton, where we paid dock dues (6/-) and were put on board the tender which took us on board the 'Para' which was lying out in Southampton water. We soon found our cabin (150/4) which was a very nice room in the fore part of the ship, with two berths and a sofa. Into this we had our luggage carried & we took out things we immediately required & went on the Quarterdeck to see what was going on. There were a jolly number of people – many of whom were friends of passengers coming to see them off. The most-troubled was a little boy about 12 yrs of age who saw his Mother off, he was crying bitterly. About 3.30 the bell rang & all for shore went on the tender – & after they had cheered us lustily we parted – they for England & we for the West Indies.

We got on board the Para soon after 12 o'clock – but we were delayed by the arrival of the mails & we did not sail until 5 minutes before 4. We went briskly along – but the weather was a little hazy – to see the coast of the I of Wight cliffs. We sat down to dinner about 5.30 & enjoyed it. Went to bed early about 8 o'clock, I slept well.

Sunday Sept 18th

Got up about 8 o'clock & felt rather qualmish. Lizzie had some tea & was sick after it. I drank none & was sick without. But we had not much sickness all day Sunday. We were on deck most of the time but we took no food whatsoever. Went to bed about quarter past 7 o'clock. It was rather squally in the night and & the ship rolled a little.

Monday Sept 19th

Very qualmish – much sickness. Went on deck & remained there the greatest part of the time until about 5.30. Then went to bed. Got more squally towards night & the rolling of the ship was worse. I took no food all day.

Tuesday Sept 20th

Felt ill, remained in bed. Living on ice & iced water and lemonade. Ice was by far the best stuff for it. When I had plenty of ice it felt quite comfortable. Lizzie remained in bed Tuesday, Wednesday altogether but was up for a part of the day on Thursday. Had some hot beef tea.

Wednesday Sept 21st

At last – was much better though with no food.

Thursday Sept 22nd

Got up early. Had 3 eggs for breakfast and some iced water and bread – Lizzie in bed but with some food. I dined and lunched in the saloon. Had hot bath.

Friday Sept 23rd

Had a sea and shower bath. Glowing. Sea has been smooth since yesterday, no rolling. Delightful weather. Warm breeze on deck, no rain. We had very heavy rain on Tuesday & Wednesday. Very hungry.

Lizzie lunched in the saloon today. Has been on deck all day.

I never had a better night's sleep than last night.

Lizzie did not feel so well in the evening, did not go into dinner. I ate a very hearty dinner.

Lizzie went to bed early – I went about 9.30. Hot night. The weather is getting hot – but there is a beautiful breeze on deck and amid ships where the hatches are open.

Saturday Sept 24th

Got up early and had a bath – but felt qualmish all day. Went in to breakfast and lunch though but not to dinner. Lizzie has been qualmish all day and sick several times. Had some hot soup made for Lizzie, & she was better towards night. Went to bed early 6.30, slept through the best part of the night. Lizzie had a pretty good night.

Sunday Sept 25th

Got up early & had a bath and went up walking on the quarter deck for several hours before breakfast. Lizzie much better. Has taken a good deal of beef jelly, looks better, less qualmish & no sickness. I went & had breakfast & then church at 10.30, where the archdeacon read the Litany and preached a short sermon. Went to lunch and then there was some hymn singing in the afternoon.

There was some singing again in the evening. Went to bed early.

Sunday Oct 2nd

We had service in the morning, read by the captain. It was a very hot day one of the hottest we have had. Very fine, and the sea as smooth as a lake. Lizzie spent the great part of the day on deck – but in the afternoon she went down to the saloon, as it was cooler there.

The diary then skips several days and we learn that the ship has landed safely in Jamaica. It is noticeable how little he writes about Lizzie now that he can no longer play doctor to her.

Thursday Oct 27th
Started with Mr D at 9.30 to see the shrine in the Valley. Went on a pretty ride along the slopes and on the leeward side – passed through several negro villages – little huts – until we got to the valley. There Mr D had to marry a nice couple. A boy went with me and showed me Mr Edward Phillips' house – a preacher, a Blackman about 45 yrs of age, he gave me a drink of coconut which was very good. He rode with me to the shrine which is situated about a mile up the valley, close to the beacon. It is a very large purple red structure with an inclined face towards the river.

The highest part of this shrine is about 8 feet high.

We afterwards called on Mr H – the manager of the Rutland Estate – then returned to wish Mr Philips goodbye and rode to meet Mr L – met him on the ridge and then rode to Kingston together – which we reached at 3.30.

Mr Hazell – Mr and Mrs Hughes & Mr Brauch dined at Mr L's this evening. Mr Brauch's son wants to become a doctor & Mr Hazell's son is going to be a Barrister.

Friday Oct 28th
Rode with Mr McL to see the spa and drink the water. It is a powerful opening in the S Valley – built around with bricks. I was told it was chalky water but I found it was nothing of the sort. The water is like London water and very nice.

We sailed about 7 in the evening, got to Barbados about 6 in the morning – after a very smooth journey.

The diary entries are sparse and repetitive for a few days, with more details of seasickness and occasional meals, before John Williams is able to say he is better once more.

Sunday Nov 6th
My birthday. Lizzie is still qualmish.

Sunday night at 9 o'clock was beautiful – and we went to bed thinking we were going to get beautiful weather.

Monday Nov 7th
Wind and sea more about 4 inches this evening – and it blew a severe gale all day and Monday night. The stern of the vessel dipped under the waves.

Tuesday Nov 8th
Wakening at 9 o'clock with wind and sea subsided and we had a beautiful day.

Wednesday Nov 9th
Beautiful day. Both well.

Thursday Nov 10th
Lizzie for first time at breakfast. Beautiful day.

The writing in these extracts does not suggest a passionate marriage. The man who wrote to 'Sophia' Owen was altogether different from the one who wrote about his wife's seasickness in his diary of their trip to the West Indies.

In 1883 Williams started work as physician at the General Lying-In Hospital in York Road, Lambeth, and the following year (together with his friend Dr Francis Champneys) he took over control of the hospital; according to John Williams, they did a very good job. They managed to bring levels of the mortality rate amongst women down to almost zero, principally through applying the antiseptic procedures pioneered by Sir Joseph Lister.

It was just as well that his hospital practice was flourishing, for his private practice, as before, occasionally struggled. In his obituary published in the *Lancet*, the writer notes that 'although at first John Williams was not very successful in private work it was obvious to his colleagues that his ability was outstanding'. It is tempting to continue to attribute this to a poor bedside manner, or to snobbery related to his upbringing, but we are also afforded a further glimpse from an article about him published in a magazine, the *Gentlewoman*, in 1891. Here, the anonymous author suggests he is somewhat dour – 'he will never set the Thames on fire' – that he is aggressively vain, eschews subtlety, neglects simple courtesies towards his patients, and that there is about him more 'promise than performance'. Of course this article was written after the events of 1888, which seemed to have changed him irrevocably, but 'neglecting courtesies' appeared to be entirely in keeping with what we knew about him from the start of his career. As we had learned from the obituaries, the outpouring of affection after his death showed that Dr Williams could command the respect of his peers and colleagues; but that he was rarely able to engender affection in his patients.

John Williams's attitude to his patients can be seen from his comments in the proceedings of the Obstetrical Society. In one case, he recommends letting a disease run its course so that the doctor in charge could usefully comment upon its progress at future meetings – which shows scant concern for the patient. In another, he lists the frequency of applications 'of electricity' given to a woman, then to the douches of 'foaming nitric acid' that are applied to wash out her uterus. 'It caused a great deal of pain,' he nonchalantly remarks.

But meanwhile it was away from the privileged West End that John Williams's thoughts were turning. Indication of this can be seen in the proceedings of the Obstetrical Society, where he made it clear that he was familiar with a different class of woman than he would have seen both at his private practice and at UCH. Firstly, he made a remark regarding Jewish women. At the time, the largest Jewish population in London was in Whitechapel, and John Williams declared, when discussing the nature of the Mosaic law's stipulation about the length of time women were said to be 'unclean' during their periods, that he 'had made many enquiries of Jewesses upon this point'. Secondly, when presenting a paper to the society on the nature of the corroding ulcers of the '*os uterii*' (the 'mouth of the womb'), one of the fellows identified these ulcers as those 'occurring in the intemperate, half-starved prostitutes found in the lowest slums of the Thames District'. We already knew that he worked closely with Dr Francis Champneys (whose father was the rector of St Mary's in Whitechapel until 1851), but we learned through reading the records at the Obstetrical Society that the two of them worked just as closely with Dr Herman of the London Hospital, now the Royal London, prominently situated in the Whitechapel Road. Both these doctors co-authored papers with John Williams, and were his supporters at the Obstetrical Society.

By the mid 1880s, Dr John Williams was working at four institutions: University College Hospital in Gower Street; the Lying-In Hospital and the Royal Infirmary, both in Lambeth (and not far from the workhouse infirmary where Mary Ann Nichols was living in early 1888); and the St Pancras and Northern Dispensary, around the corner from UCH in the Euston Road. In addition, he was voted President of the Obstetrical Society in 1887, and he was both Professor and Examiner in Midwifery at University College. To cap it all, in late 1887 he was appointed by one of Queen Victoria's children, Princess Beatrice, to be her personal physician *accoucheur*; overseeing her pregnancy and childbirth. He was recommended for the post by his old friend Dr William Jenner (who, as Dean in 1872, had been responsible for appointing John to UCH in the first place), and he rapidly made himself indispensable to the Princess. Princess Beatrice was married to Prince Henry of Battenburg and had met John Williams at University College Hospital, but this appointment raised the same mutterings as before, when John Williams was originally taken on at UCH.

Closer to home, a private matter was preoccupying John Williams. His wife, it would seem, was unable to have children. Given his arrogance, it is safe to assume that he never for one moment thought that the failure of the marriage to produce children might have been because of him. Instead we can observe, from outside the marriage, the changes this disappointment wrought upon Lizzie. From being the plump, cheery-looking girl seen in her youthful photograph, she became thin, browbeaten, and altogether a shadow of her former self. Her husband's intense interest in genealogy was underpinned by a more personal determination to replace his dead older brother David, and ensure that the Williams family line continued. His brother Morgan remained unmarried, and Nathaniel, who married the year after John, was never to have children, in contrast to the other side of the family who seemed to produce cousins in large numbers.

Lizzie Hughes had a sad life. Her mother died when she was young and she married a man older than her, who, all the evidence suggests, did not really cherish her as much as she might have wished. Even after their trip, which was maybe meant to be a 'second honeymoon', she failed to produce the children they both craved. For some reason – be it this mutual disappointment, or maybe she was suffering from some illness – her husband never fully integrated her into his life. It was interesting to learn that she did not attend important events with him. He had persuaded her to marry him – presumably her father, impressed by his future son-in-law, helped press his case – but there appears more of a sense of duty in the marriage than love. If some illness prevented her from having children, maybe the depression that ensued drove them further apart. Maybe a sense of marital duty was enough for Lizzie, but it was clearly not enough for her husband.

We know from his records that John was obsessed by genealogy. He put a tremendous amount of work not only into his own lineage but also his wife's, as if he was tracing the absence of issue through the bloodline. It is reasonable to assume, from the intensity of his relationship with his mother (matched only by that of Nathaniel's), that he wanted to see everything she had achieved continued through the generations. A remark by Ruth Evans, his biographer, confirms his unhappiness: 'the one great sadness of his life was that he had no children'.

Chapter Seven

What kind of doctor was John Williams? The best source of material, at least in as much as he presented it, was in the *Transactions of the Obstetrical Society*, the official record of the Society of Obstetricians and Gynaecologists, of which he was a prominent member – indeed, later on, its President. The minutes in the *Transactions* were fascinating. It was obvious that he was highly thought of by his colleagues; and yet those who disagreed with him were numerous, and they made their objections known. Was this because of simple snobbery? Was he looked down upon because he was Welsh? Or was it because of something else? Were they envious of his successes?

Going through the volumes of the *Transactions* from 1875, when John Williams was elected to the council of the society, up to the time he was President, it was clear that there were certain protocols that had to be followed. Each season began with the President's address: he would outline aspects of the profession and its development that he felt most deserved notice, and usually take the opportunity to draw attention to his own research. Thereafter he would be expected to make the first reply to the papers delivered to the society by one of its fellows, and often to sum up the argument at the end of the discussion that followed. Finally, he would direct his fellows as to who should dissect the deformed foetuses and other materials presented to the society which formed part of their discussions.

However, John Williams was never as popular a fellow or President as others around him – Dr Francis Champneys, for instance, who was clearly well liked and is accorded respect in books about obstetrics even today. John Williams, on the other hand, was scorned by some of his colleagues, and, when he took issue with the proposition put forward in Dr Dakin's 'Sarcometous Uterus removed by Vaginal Hysterectomy' paper in April 1890, was shouted down by all the fellows present – Dr Macnaughton-Jones called John Williams's views 'fallacious'. No other President of the society seemed to be criticised in the way that John Williams was – yet he seemed to thrive on these attacks, as if they confirmed for him that he was right.

Much of the criticism was probably unfair, as it came from those who were reluctant to put into practice the kind of protocols that had become standard then, such as the practice of 'Listerism' which John Williams, along with Dr Champneys, championed. The fuddy-duddies within the profession were determined to resist these newfangled ways, and looked all the more foolish for it. Perhaps it is wrong to see these attacks in such simple terms; but elsewhere the same sort of reaction to him as a colleague was evident. In the archive of UCH, the minutes of the meeting in 1893, at which John Williams's retirement from active duty at the hospital was also announced, record his appointment as a consultant. No letter of resignation from him was read out, as was customary, and, more importantly, no vote of thanks for his work was taken.

Among the items in John Williams's archive in the National Library in Aberystwyth was a copy of an article dated 15 August 1891 from a magazine called the *Gentlewoman*. This is fascinating because it provides an opinion of John Williams as a practitioner, from an independent source. The article was part of a series, entitled 'Medicos under the Microscope', and many doctors before Williams had come under the author's scrutiny. The article provides insights that are not found in any other source, but the context is not clear. It was important to consult other copies of the magazine; not only for what it said about Williams, but also at the magazine itself – was this piece in keeping with the rest of the magazine? And were the opinions expressed here about Williams similar to those about others?

The *Gentlewoman* can be read at the British Library's newspaper archive at Colindale, a grim-looking building in north London. The library is an extraordinary mine of material, and real, not microfilmed, copies of the paper are a joy to look at. All the original advertisements, everything from soap to stays, nestle alongside the instructive and patronising text. Articles on the law (by 'Portia') and on the city (by 'Cassandra'), sit alongside more gossipy pieces such as 'Cosy Corner Chat' which fills two or three pages with nonsense such as:

Just fancy this!
There are between 36,000,000 and 37,000,000 born in the world every year, that is at the rate of about 70 per minute, more than one for every beat of the clock.
Poor little things!

Skipping past 'Famous People I Have Met', the tone of some of the magazine is summed up by a heading 'French Books That May Be Read'. This however, was at odds with some of the regular articles – those on the city and on the law – which set out to be useful rather than simply judgemental. This was obviously the aim of 'Medicos under the Microscope': 'next week,' the magazine announced in January 1891, 'will appear the first of a series of articles under the above heading, a list that comprises the Galahads of the profession.' The series would cover general practitioners, surgeons, specialists and obstetricians. The anonymous author – who signed herself, in Greek, 'Microscopist' – pointed to existing rules, which forbade doctors from advertising. This, she felt, justified the publication of such a series of quick portraits, as it gave their readers both an idea of what was felt about other doctors in London and elsewhere, and an insight into how their own doctor was seen. The articles were written, the subheading continued, 'with a full knowledge of the Laws, written and unwritten, which forbid Doctors to adopt any of the ordinary forms of publicity'. The writer goes on to say, 'the Medical Men included in this series have not been invited to sit for their pen portraits. But the pictures will not be any the less true to life because their subjects have no hand in their preparation, nor even knowledge of their production.'

Unsurprisingly perhaps, the series attracted a great deal of criticism from the medical press, though having read all the articles in the series it is hard to see why. Almost all of them are flattering, with one or two exceptions: William Playfair, in the 1 August 1891 issue, and John Williams, in the 15 August 1891 issue, are the only two doctors who merit anything negative from 'Microscopist'.

The article about John Williams is worth quoting in full as it tells us a lot about Dr Williams that we have no other source for. Apart from being an independent point of view, it is, perhaps more importantly, a woman's point of view – when almost all the other tributes and recollections we have of him are from men. Although of course Queen Victoria's tributes to him are fulsome, he was surely on his best behaviour with her. 'Microscopist' and others like her saw a different side to the doctor. A highly revealing note scribbled by Williams on the top of the article says, 'I should like to have met Microscopist. She must have been a little girl I think.'

Opposite
This is the copy of the *Gentlewoman* magazine found in Sir John Williams's archive. It carries his own notes, along with some scribbles from the person who sent him the article in the first place. 'Microscopist' was the pseudonym used by the author of the piece.

*This was sent to me by some
one together with the margi-
notes. I should like to have the
names of ... ... have been
a little full I think* JW

AUGUST 15, 1891.

Medicos under the Microscope.

@ @ @ @ @ @

*This unique series of articles has been written for the sole purpose
of forming a useful guide to our lady readers, and with a full
knowledge of the Laws, written and unwritten, which forbid
Doctors to adopt any of the ordinary forms of publicity. It
must be clearly understood that the Medical Men included in this
series have not been invited to sit for their pen portraits. But
the pictures will not be any the less true to life because the
subjects have had no hand in their preparation, nor even
knowledge of their production.*

Specialists.

DR. JOHN WILLIAMS, M.D., F.R.C.P.

DR. JOHN WILLIAMS is a very difficult man with whom to
deal. He presents a combination of qualities so unusual
that it requires greater space than I have at my command to do him justice.

There is no use in attempting to disguise the fact that
there exists a prejudice against Dr. Williams. It is intangible perhaps, hard to analyse, but, like hydra-headed
scandal, it is equally hard to kill. It is best to grapple
with it boldly, drag it to light, and see what effect free
ventilation will have upon it.

John Williams commenced his professional life as a
general practitioner at Swansea. From this somewhat lowly position he was suddenly, and to the
surprise of London medical circles, appointed
to a vacancy on the staff of King's College Hospital.
Envious colleagues whispered of "wire-pulling;" those
who, apparently, were well informed were prepared with
details. It remained to Sir William Jenner to explain,
and Sir Wm. Jenner did not explain. This was the beginning of the bitterness which has since dominated the
intercourse between Dr. Williams and a certain section of
his colleagues. More was to follow, equally vague,
equally indefinite. He was created accoucheur to H.R.H.
Princess Beatrice. Why? The envious ones could not
understand it, they cannot understand it now, and the
fact that Dr. John Williams' name is so frequently
before the public has but increased their chagrin. It
has also increased his practice. There are people so
curiously constituted, that it gives them a real pleasure
to be associated with Royalty, even in the distant
and slender way of having the same medical attendant.
It is perhaps true that Dr. Williams has profited by the
snobbishness of the British public, but is he to be held
responsible for this?

I am no blind partisan of Dr. Williams. I am ...

Dr John Williams is a very difficult man with whom to deal. He presents a combination of qualities so unusual that it requires greater space than I have at my command to do him justice.

There is no use in attempting to disguise the fact that here exists a prejudice against Dr Williams. It is intangible perhaps, hard to analyse, but, like hydra-headed scandal, it is equally hard to kill. It is best to grapple with it boldly, drag it to light, and see what effect free ventilation will have upon it.

John Williams commenced his professional life as a general practitioner at Swansea. From this somewhat lowly position he was suddenly, and to the surprise of London medical circles, appointed to a vacancy on the staff of King's College Hospital. Envious colleagues whispered of 'wire-pulling'; those who, apparently, were well informed were prepared with details. It remained to Sir William Jenner to explain, and Sir Wm Jenner did not explain. This was the beginning of the bitterness which has since dominated the intercourse between Dr Williams and a certain section of his colleagues. More was to follow, equally vague, equally indefinite. He was created *Accoucheur* to HRH Princess Beatrice. Why? The envious ones could not understand it, they cannot understand it now, and the fact that Sir John Williams's name is so frequently before the public has but increased their chagrin. It has also increased his practice. There are people so curiously constituted that it gives them a real pleasure to be associated with Royalty, even in the distant and slender way of having the same medical attendant. It is perhaps true that Dr Williams has profited by the snobbishness of the British public, but is he to be held responsible for this?

I am no blind partisan of Dr Williams. I admit that he has not established by any valuable book, new discovery of brilliant cure, a claim to be considered as the leading London obstetrician. But for all that I am prepared to assert that he is an able man, resourceful and practical, level-headed in an emergency, cool and wide awake. Her Royal Highness knew what she was about. If he will never set the Thames on fire, he will at least never admit his abortive attempts to compass that conflagration. His reticence is a valuable quality; that he relaxes it a little when on the subject of his position and influence is, to my way of thinking, the only regrettable feature in his character.

He has been conspicuously successful with the public; he is making a large income; other men are not. This is the *crux* of the whole thing, and 'it is a jealous people'.

I admit there are men who are equally successful who are not equally unpopular. But Dr Williams has not the *suaviter in modo*. If he wants to say that he does not care to undertake gynaecological operations, he is not content with a modest hint on the subject. A graceful retirement from a portion of his practice, never onerous, is not the course he pursues. He asserts himself aggressively. He issues a letter, a sort of royal proclamation, and to enforce its importance he signs it conjointly with Dr Champneys. But when so much is admitted, it must be confessed it was a very venial crime, not deserving of the burst of indignation that followed. From another man it would have been laughed at and forgotten.

That he models himself upon the traditions of Dr Matthews Duncan, that he is a Jesuit, that he is blatantly vain and inordinately dogmatic, are assertions that may be at once dismissed. The old adage of the chain and its weakest link suffices for them all. Dr John Williams, far from being a Jesuit, is a Welsh Methodist, almost its exact antithesis! So much for the demon Rumour.

The simply furnished reception room at 63 Brook Street, is usually full of ladies, who cast surreptitiously inquiring glances at each other, and seem to be engaged in a species of mild mental arithmetic. A husky parrot with a distressing cough relieves the monotony of waiting and endeavours feebly to say a few words. But ornothologically considered, it is not to be mentioned in the same way with the bird of like species possessed by Dr David Ferrier [who owns a 'lively, beautiful' parrot who calls out that it is 'poorly' all the time].

When the patient reaches the consulting-room, after a dignified wait, she finds herself in a light and cheerful room – commodious, staid, and simple. Sometimes Dr Williams rises with benignant courtesy, but sometimes his brow is overladen with care, and he is studiously abrupt. These are the times when, so to speak, dynasties are in his hands, and common mortals sink into insignificance. He is handsome, prosperous, portly, on first impression. Later, one discovers that he is not quite handsome, his lips are a thought too full, his eyes are too weakly blue. Not quite prosperous – or why those tell-tale lines? Not quite portly – the ample proportions are more promise than performance. He is not quite convincing, he is not quite impressive, but he is very near both those standards. His hair is grey, his close trimmed whiskers grey also. His hands are white and well-cared for, he dresses well, his voice, though a little hard sometimes, is pleasant. All the time one talks to him, one wonders, 'why don't they like him?' And there is no answer, or if there be one, it is not known to

'Microscopist'

There are many extraordinary things in this article, not the least of which is its tone, compared to the other articles – none of them, not even the one about Dr Playfair, is so antagonistic towards its subject. But it adds to what has already been uncovered about him; for instance, he has chosen not to perform 'operations', *even in private practice* – as we later learned that he had asked not to at UCH. Furthermore, he sent out a letter to tell every one of his patients this news. This led to a suspicion – that he had carried out 'ovariotomies' on the streets of Whitechapel, and now no longer could trust himself. The writer's clever style of proposing questions, which she then corrects, allows her to put forward fairly rude opinions – that he is vain and dogmatic – while denying the least important of them, that he is a Jesuit.

Then there is the interesting passage about those 'common mortals' who sometimes feel snubbed by him. Bearing in mind that this is in his private practice, and he relied upon these patients to pay for him and his lifestyle, it is surprising that he carried on as he did. If he was prepared to treat paying patients in this way, he would be more than ready to be brusque and even harsh with those who came to him in the expectation of being treated for nothing.

And then there is the question of the 'tell-tale lines' that he carries; the writer thinks this may be because he is worried about money, but as we know he amassed a considerable fortune and collected an enormous number of rare books and manuscripts. So his worry lines came from something else, something of which the writer knows nothing.

The article ends in a different way from all the others we read. In every other case, the author concluded with a list of the doctor's publications but not in this instance. And, strangely, '*Microscopist*' ended all her other pieces properly, not, as here, with an unpunctuated final sentence.

In the archive at the National Library are copies of some of the papers that he had written, and we thought it would be useful to look more widely at how his peer group reacted to them.

For example, if you consult the *Lancet* and the *British Medical Journal* – best done at the Wellcome Library in London – his name does not come up that frequently. There are accounts of some of his achievements in other books, though not always to his benefit. In *Historical Review of British Obstetrics and Gynaecology*, edited by J. M. Munro Kerr and others, it says:

Sir John Williams in 1883 successfully removed a right ovarian cyst from a patient in labour with her fourth child. In his account of the case, he seems to have been more interested in the slow involution of the uterus than in the fact that he was recording what was apparently the first ovariotomy during labour to be performed in Great Britain.

Ovariotomy – 'the excision of the ovary' – was an important operation in those days but it was only when looking at Ann Dally's book about the history of surgery, *Women Under the Knife*, that it is possible to see quite how important it was considered to be:

> The operation of ovariotomy gradually became accepted as the operation by which a surgeon's skill and worth were assessed. Almost any description of a surgeon in the second part of the nineteenth century informs the reader of the date when he 'did his first ovariotomy'. Clearly it was regarded as an important milestone in a surgeon's career.

Recent histories of surgery suggest that it was women on whom doctors chose to refine the skills required to achieve a level of fame in their profession. At the same time, the practice and study of gynaecology developed, a time noted by Ann Dally as 'the very period of maximum prejudice against women, when attitudes towards them were at their most bizarre, in a curious mixture of contempt and idealisation'. She goes on to say that gynaecology was not an obvious choice for many medical students to follow:

> Gynaecology tends to be messy and smelly. To practise it with interest and pleasure requires a training, a certain orientation and also specific equipment. Probably most doc-

tors of both sexes have always had to overcome an initial distaste and reluctance to become involved in it.

She quotes from a book *Medical Chaos and Crime* by Norman Barnesby published in 1910 which goes much further:

Perversion plays a part in surgery, and especially gynaecology, never before suspected, finding therein a license and security possible in no other legalized profession or occupation.

Nothing available makes it clear what motivated John Williams to be an obstetrician, and to become the President of the Society of Obstetricians and Gynaecologists as part of his climb up the slippery slope of success, but it is certain that he was no sexual pervert. He was motivated, the evidence indicates, by a genuine desire to understand and conquer the diseases that fascinated him, *by whatever means at his disposal.*

Even the articles about his death revealed little about the research he undertook. Among the fullest entries in the *Lancet* was the obituary for John Williams, published on 5 June 1926. The most revealing comment remains – that he found it hard to become established in private work, and that it was only thanks to his colleagues who helped to get him started that he took this route. This detail was recalled despite being over fifty years after he had supposedly been struggling in private work. His difficulties, then, were of an order of magnitude that had not been fully appreciated.

But one of the most helpful books, partly because it confirms John Williams's absence from UCH around the time we believed him to be elsewhere, and partly because it yet again underlines the (at best) dismissive attitude of Victorian doctors to their subjects, was a catalogue that John Williams himself compiled.

One of the chief reasons why doctors were prepared to work at teaching hospitals such as UCH was because they were able to carry out research there. At UCH, a museum of 'specimens' illustrating their work aided this research, allowing students, as much as their teachers, to study . In 1891, John Williams, together with the Curator of the Museum, Charles Stonham, compiled a *Descriptive Catalogue of the Specimens Illustrating the Pathology of Gynaecology and Obstetric Medicine Contained in the Museum of University College, London.* This catalogue runs to about seventy pages and is divided into seven sections:

Diseases of the Ovaries
Diseases of the Fallopian Tubes
Diseases of the Uterus
Diseases of the Vagina and External Organs of Generation
The Anatomy of Pregnancy
Injuries and Diseases incidental to Gestation and Parturition
Malformation of the Foetus

Entries within each section consist of a few lines of description, and are sometimes followed by an italicised passage outlining the patient's history and giving dates and places of removal of the exhibited part. Much of it makes for unpleasant reading. At first, John Williams's language seems quite cold, but it is soon apparent that it is simply observational; that is, until he describes the 'papillomata covering the surface of the ovary' and describes it as 'a beautiful specimen'. The writer also appears devoid of compassion for the patient: when he describes a prolapsed uterus so inverted that 'it comes to lie outside the vulva', he records that 'the exposed part becomes, after a time, quite altered in character'. And painful, too, perhaps?

But Dr Williams's emotions were occasionally engaged. In a note about a woman who had been treated at UCH for eight years before her death, he writes: 'When dying, she requested that her body might be examined in order to satisfy her friends that she had been, during the early part of her disorder, the subject of unfounded suspicions and aspersions.' John Williams sees fit to record this in a document intended for his fellow physicians. This was not just a catalogue for research: Dr Williams was also justifying, through his words, the work of anatomists.

There were other smaller points to be drawn from this book. Some of the items in the museum were from private patients treated by John Williams; the 'uterus with sarcoma' of 4137a, for example. This woman, thirty-eight years old, had been seeing John Williams for three years. Would a respectable private patient expect parts of her body to be on display in a university's museum? It was far more likely that this was a patient from the poorer part of town, a patient that Dr Williams saw while in Whitechapel. Her uterus would simply arrive at UCH in a jar in the doctor's hands, he would tell those who enquired that it came from a private patient – and no one would be any the wiser.

He expands upon cases that he himself was involved with, such as the patient who had a cyst so large that 'two or three pailfuls of fluid were removed' from it (the patient died). But amongst these examples of John Williams performing 'heroic' surgical acts lie two crucial pieces of information. Items 4122 and 4091 were removed from two female patients on 31 August and 25 September 1888 respectively – but not by John Williams. He dutifully records that they were removed by his assistant, Dr Herbert Spencer. The items removed were taken, *according to the notes made by John Williams*, from Emma Wood, who had her uterus and bladder removed; and Fanny Wright, who also had her uterus and bladder removed. Both women died. So where was Dr John Williams then, and what was so important about those particular dates?

On 31 August, Mary Ann Nichols was killed. Both Liz Stride and Catherine Eddowes died on 30 September. John Williams, through the pages of the *Descriptive Catalogue*, had confirmed that he was not at UCH at the time of Mary Ann Nichols's death, and that he was also absent at around the time that Catherine Eddowes and Liz Stride were murdered.

*

A clearer portrait was beginning to form of John Williams as a doctor in the hospital; but what sort of man was he to his private, and wealthy patients? He was not popular with all his patients, but he had been too successful in his professional career for it to be possible to make a judgment without looking at the one area of his working life that shows him in a different light. The society women of London, and the princesses of the royal family, had found him to be a truly excellent doctor.

One picture of his private career was provided by some letters sent by John Williams in his capacity as doctor, held in the archive of the Asquith family kept in the Bodleian Library in Oxford. Margot Asquith – who wrote in her autobiography that she had visited factory girls in Whitechapel in 1888 – became a patient of John Williams in the 1890s. These letters give a rare glimpse of what it was like for a private patient to have him as a doctor; and the tone of some of the letters that he wrote to her over the years is surprising. He continued to write to her until after the First World War, and his last letter gives details of the visit paid to the National Library by some of her stepchildren, including Lady Bonham Carter.

Margot's first pregnancy, which resulted in a stillbirth, was a very difficult one and 'it was entirely owing to his [John Williams's] skill that she survived at all,' says Colin Clifford in his biography of the Asquiths published in 2002. The doctor told her to rest in bed for six weeks, after which she left London to return to her home at Glen in Scotland. In the letter that he then wrote to her some weeks later, John Williams appears more like a lover than a doctor. The strength of emotion is undeniable for someone who, up until now, had appeared a fairly dry and distant person – particularly so, given that he had recently delivered the woman of a dead child.

Once again, we puzzled our way through his handwriting, but had to concede defeat with some words. The 'little children' he refers to are her stepchildren, from Herbert Asquith's first marriage.

31 July 1895

Dear Child,

I trust the journey north did not over-fatigue you and that you reached Glen none the worse for it. Your advent there must have been hailed with pleasure by everyone, especially by the little children who must have been delighted to have their Margot with them again. The period of convalescence after an illness in this dismal place can never be anything but depressing, and you must have found it very much so since its frequent [maddening?] drawback. I wish you could have bounded into health at once – but at Glen you will find it very difficult. You will recover strength by leaps and bounds and the air of Scotland will soon bring back the roses to your pale cheeks.

Do not think – do not brood at any rate – over the past – but look to what is to come, and that with a brave and cheerful heart. Brave you have been, and more I know you will be, and a time will come when you will be amply rewarded. I cannot tell you how much I feel indebted to you for all your patience, [?], faith, goodness and trustfulness. A sense of pleasure will always prevail over all others when ever I shall look back upon the time during which I have known you – a time (forgetful and negligent as I am) which cannot pass out of my memory. You have given me a new pleasure in life, and in watching you and your husband (and I shall watch you) and the part you play in moulding the future of the country. I shall have a new and [?] interest. You gave me this.

I hope you found Sir Charles well, please to convey to him expressions of my high esteem, tell your husband that I shall expect to see your real self in October and believe that I am devoted to you [?], J.W.

The letter that follows in the collection is all the more remarkable because of what precedes it. Written some five years later, John Williams is still in Brook Street, but his humour is worse; and although he is evidently still good friends with Margot Asquith, the warmth of his earlier communication is missing. The tone – from the way he addresses her, through to the way he signs off the letter – is radically different from that of the earlier letter.

25 Nov 1900

Dear Mrs Asquith,
I do not know, nor have I any wish to know, indeed I would rather not know, what my [inquisitor?] told you of my wife, but I gather that it was something the reverse of complimentary. Fortunately I am almost if not quite indifferent as to the opinions of most people about me and mine – and on this point I think that I am quite indifferent. There are two things that are always welcome to me: opposition to abuse: anything that is offensive – praise which produces [largesse?] and general [vileness?]: one thing that at our time would have been intolerable, crushing neglect. I cannot complain of the last. Here ends all thought of your letter.

Oddly I have during the last fortnight been troubled beyond measure by the foolish and wicked talk of so called friends respecting a friend of mine now dead. I have had to speak and write much with a view to try and stop the tongues of scandal which under the circumstances should have been absolutely silent. Success however was very partial, and the words of the sturdy old thinker 'the poison of an asp is other than lawful [?]' have often occurred to me as often [?] as the modern rendering [?] 'Speak no slander, nor listen to it.' The morbid state of mind which is so common is I believe greatly on the increase and this increase is largely due to the penny press. O for a heavy box of paper.

Many thanks for *Napoleon*. I shall read it with pleasure at least for the sake of the sender [?] as I had it not. Nor did I intend to obtain it, because I was not favourably impressed by the notices of it I had seen in the papers. Nor has Napoleonology [?] been a favourite study with me.

Yours always very truly

John Williams

What had been said about Lizzie? Who had said it? On what grounds? Was this the confirmation that we had been looking for all along, that there was something wrong in his marriage about which we were never going to know more? Who was this friend whom he felt he had to defend? Could it be anyone we've already read about? Against what sort of attacks? The slander that should have been 'silent' – was this something he was only too well aware of himself? Unfortunately, this is a mystery that cannot be solved – no other letters in the collection remain that could clarify the identity of the person any further.

None of the later letters returns to this theme. They are either pleas for her to visit him in Aberystwyth, or letters encouraging her husband – by then Prime Minister – to greater things. One letter, dated 26 August 1912, refers to 'little Anthony' (who grew up to be a successful film director) and recalls something of his own childhood:

When I was his age I had to walk three miles to school and three miles back daily without home lessons and I have every reason to think that it was best for the development of my physical strength.

Later that year he writes that 'I am fairly well but I am getting to love idleness – a new trait in me – I do not like it for I think that there is nothing like work.' The busy doctor of the late 1880s was always active, and worked all the time; but not in the years that immediately followed after that.

But the Asquiths were far from being the only brush with high society that John Williams enjoyed. The *Lancet* of 17 March 1888 carried the following announcement: 'HRH Princess Beatrice, Princess Henry of Battenburg, has been pleased to appoint John Williams, MD, to be physician *accoucheur* to Her Royal Highness.'

Princess Beatrice was married to Prince Henry of Battenburg, and, before John Williams was appointed to be her physician *accoucheur*, they had had two children together. The two eldest were Alexander, born on 23 November 1886, and Victoria Eugenie, born on 24 October 1887, who went on to become Queen of Spain and died in 1969. John Williams was in attendance at the birth of Leopold (born in 1889; he died before John Williams, in 1922), and Maurice, born in 1891, who also died young, in 1914.

Princess Beatrice was Queen Victoria's youngest daughter and was known as 'Baby' to her mother. Like Victoria, Beatrice suffered the early death of her husband, and, having spent most of her youth at her mother's side, went on to spend a large part of her adult life with her as well. She was entrusted by Victoria with the task of compiling and preparing for publication the Queen's journals and letters, and naturally she removed passages she felt posterity need not know about. Luckily for historians, however, the Queen and Prince Albert had foreseen this, and had privately printed some material already – so giving us insights into Victoria's feelings on her wedding night, for instance.

But 'Baby' did something else for her mother. She introduced her to John Williams, and in the last years of the Queen's life the Welsh doctor was to become a support for her and her family. John Williams had already proved his worth to the royal family not only with Princess Beatrice, but also with her brother's daughter-in-law, the Duchess of York (and later Queen Mary), whom he first attended in 1894.

It was immediately clear that the royal family held John Williams in high esteem, and that he played his role as the atten-

John Williams as a young boy: 'I look back upon this period of my life not only as one of the pleasantest and brightest but also as one of the best spent.'

John Williams's mother, Elinor, who ran the family farm in Wales where he grew up, after her husband died. John Williams referred to her as 'my guide'.

John Williams as a student doctor in London. A successful student at
University College Hospital, he returned to Wales to be a general practitioner
in Swansea.

John Williams had three brothers: David, the eldest, who died young, Morgan Williams, seen here, who moved to live in America, and to whom we thought John Williams had written his note about the 'clinic at Whitechapel', and …

Nathaniel Williams, the youngest son, who stayed on to work at the farm and wrote a memoir of his mother which John Williams paid to have printed.

Sir William Jenner. John Williams was taken under this man's wing, and it was thanks to Jenner that Williams both took up his post at University College Hospital and, it was said, was chosen to work with the royal family.

The young students at University College Hospital. Marcus Beck, John Williams's great friend and best man at his wedding, is at the back. John Williams stands, with knee bent, in front and to the right of him.

John Williams's wife, Mary Elisabeth Ann Hughes, 'Lizzie', when young. The photographs of her taken during their marriage show a marked physical decline.

Lizzie. Older, sadder, and clearly less happy.

A troubled Lizzie (on the right) together with a cheerful Mrs Sophia Ann Owen, the second wife of John Williams's childhood friend, the Reverend Owen. It was to her that John Williams wrote at the time of his breakdown.

Whitechapel Workhouse Infirmary in 1904. It 'stretched further than the eye could see, and seemed a standing rebuke to its poverty-stricken surroundings'.

23 Aug 1888

Dear Morgan

I am sorry that I shall not be able to meet with you on the 8th Sept I will be attending a clinic at Whitechapel. I am sorry that I could not let you know earlier.

John

John Williams's letter to 'Morgan' that started off our investigation. Identifying this clinic helped us discover the true identity of Morgan.

tive family doctor very well. Queen Victoria wrote about him being 'very quiet' and 'gentle and kind', while the future George V, when John Williams was leaving them after attending the birth of Prince John in 1905, wrote 'I shall miss him very much, he is a charming man.'

For the boy from the valleys that moment must have been one of the greatest in his life. Not only had he helped at the birth of children who would one day become kings, but he was now in a position to command the highest fees for his private work. He had secured the best possible endorsement for his services. Other members of the wider royal family wrote to Queen Victoria to thank her for recommending Dr John Williams to them. No doubt he went to visit them when they required his services – no chance of royalty, however minor, having to sit patiently in his Mayfair waiting room – and his stock would have increased enormously around London as a result.

Interestingly, another element of Williams's private life can be glimpsed through these papers. In his journals, the Duke of York would paste in the occasional newspaper clipping, and one such (in 1894) gives details of the christening of the young Prince Edward (known in the family by one of his other names, David, and later titled, after his abdication, the Duke of Windsor). In the list of those attending the christening is John Williams, but not Mrs Williams. In all the times that the doctor stayed close to the royal family, he never seemed to have taken his wife with him. It is understandable that they would not invite her when he was there to help with the birth of a child, but given the personal reaction of the Duke of York, and the fact that the christening John Williams attended was only in south-west London, in Sheen, not very far from his home, it seems odd that his wife did not go with him.

John Williams's archive in the National Library of Wales also contains telegrams, letters and other materials sent by the Queen, and some members of her family, and these can be compared with the information learned from the archives at

Windsor. There were two telegrams from Queen Victoria, addressed to him at Sandringham, oddly insistent about asking him to write and telegram her. The first was clear: this must have come to him at the time of the birth of Albert, later to be King George VI, and her message – 'Please telegraph again tonight and twice for the next 2 days – daily till the 10th day and write please daily till then' – was simply because she was so concerned about the Duchess of York and about her new baby. In the royal archives, there are copies of John Williams's replies: 18 December, 12.19 p.m.; 19 December, 10.10 a.m.; 20 December 10.17 a.m.; 21 December, 10.21 a.m.; 22 December, 1.05 p.m.; and 23 December, 11.40 a.m. They all say roughly the same thing – mother and baby doing fine.

What makes less sense is the telegram that Queen Victoria sent from Balmoral to John Williams in London in October 1895. 'Hope you will write to me again.' It is a little plaintive in tone, even pathetic. What is extraordinary is that no birth is happening or even due at that time, and therefore it would seem that the Queen is asking him to write to her not with news of grandchildren and great-grandchildren, but simply for the pleasure of hearing from him. So it seemed, until we found that he continued to correspond with other members of the family, especially those whose births he had attended. John Williams had presided at the birth of five of the children of Prince George, the Duke of York. His wife Mary, who was the Duchess of Teck before becoming Duchess of York, was formerly his brother Eddy's fiancée, before Eddy died. Incidentally, Eddy was the royal 'suspect' as far as many Ripperologists were concerned.

Edward David, the eldest, would grow up to fall in love with Mrs Simpson, an American divorcée, and abdicate before he was crowned King. Albert George, the first child delivered by John Williams, named after his great-grandfather, would grow up to take the place of his brother, albeit reluctantly, and become King through the Second World War, before the crown passed on to his daughter Elizabeth. The Princess Royal, the

Duchess of Harewood, worked as a nurse at the children's hospital in Great Ormond Street for two years. Henry would become the Duke of Gloucester and Governor General of Australia; and his brother George was rumoured to have become a drug addict and had affairs with Noel Coward among others. He became the Duke of Kent, before dying in a plane crash in 1942.

The youngest son, John, was born on 11 July 1905, like almost all his brothers and sisters except for the eldest, at York Cottage in Sandringham. His delivery took place some years after John Williams had retired from private practice, and over a decade after he had stopped working in the public hospitals, so long after he had given up practising medicine. Indeed, John Williams had abandoned living in London altogether and would have had to travel to Sandringham from Wales, in order to attend the birth of a royal baby one last time.

The boy born that night was not considered well, and, by his fourth birthday, was diagnosed as suffering from a severe kind of epilepsy. This had a profound effect on his development and he was removed from the rest of his family (who were allegedly disturbed by his fits) and lived apart from them for most of the rest of his short life. Today he is remembered as 'the lost prince'.

John Williams was to remain in contact with the boy that he had delivered until he died; in the archive of the National Library of Wales is a letter sent to John Williams, only one year before Prince John died, thanking him for the gift of a book. (John Williams sent all the children of the Duke and Duchess of York – the 'Georgiepets', as their grandparents, Edward VII and his wife, called them – Christmas presents all through their youth. They would dutifully thank him and send him Christmas cards by way of return.) The letter is from one of the Queen's ladies-in-waiting, and in it she thanks John Williams for the 'charming book' which he had sent to the Prince, and which 'has much pleased him'. Although the Prince's thanks do not come directly – Charlotte Bell, known as Lalla, the Prince's constant companion, passes them on – there is a poignant note added to the letter: 'The Queen wishes me also to thank you for your kind thought for the poor dear boy.'

Prince John died in Sandringham in 1919. Contrary to the impression received by many people, he did not spend his life hidden entirely from public view, merely the last few years of it, and there are photographs of him in John Williams's archive. There are even Christmas cards that bear his name, addressed to the doctor and signed by all the young princes and the princess. Prince John's signature is traced in black ink over pencil marks, and drawn between two pencil lines to show him where to finish the loops and curves of his writing. In other words, just what you would expect from a small child learning to write; but not from one already in his early teens.

Someone who was so familiar with the Queen, on such easy terms with her and her family, would have appeared above suspicion to those he associated with in Whitechapel and elsewhere. He had, after all, been chosen from among many to be the doctor to the Queen's beloved youngest child before the murders took place, news that would have been widely circulated in the world in which he moved.

Chapter Eight

At the beginning of 1888, John Williams went to court, to try to stop a medical instruments company called Hodge & Co. from using his name in a catalogue, making it appear as if John Williams had invented an obstetric tool that they sold. What seemed to anger the doctor more was not so much that they had used his name, as the fact that the tool was commonplace and widely used in operations already – that he was being made to look foolish rather than just greedy.

The case came before the chancery division of the high court, where John Williams was treated by the court as 'a person of great eminence in the medical profession'; but the court refused his attempts to get the case resolved without a trial. The doctor had asked for a summary judgement against Hodge & Co. to be granted by the judges, but they refused, as they felt this would create a precedent they had no legal right to grant. However, they clearly felt that John Williams was in the right. They expressed the belief that it would only go to trial 'if the defendants were foolish enough to allow it to be brought on', clearly indicating what they thought the outcome of any trial might be. John Williams was as concerned as ever about his public image and frustrated that the judge failed to do what he wanted.

John Williams embarked on 1888 in a mixed state of mind; work was all-consuming for him, he seemed to fill every waking hour with appointments, meetings, visits, operations. The Society of Obstetricians expressed its gratitude to him for putting his 'valuable time' at its disposal, thus suggesting that he used every moment of the day to work. Add to this the pressure that even a seemingly harmless court case can bring – especially to one who values public opinion so highly, and not just for reasons to do with his work – and we can begin to appreciate the mental state he was in.

After the autumn of 1888, and over the next few years, John Williams cut himself adrift from the past, a little bit at a time. He requested that he be allowed to stop performing 'ovariotomies', and he stood down from various committees at UCH. In 1893, he retired altogether from the active staff at UCH, citing ill-health as one of the reasons, though he lived for a further thirty-three years. He was made Consultant Obstetric Physician of the hospital, and in 1894 received royal recognition of his role, when he was created a baronet. He adopted the motto *Bydd Gyfiawn ac nac ofna*, which translates as 'Be just and fear not'. Sir John Williams and his wife Lizzie moved into Sir William Jenner's old home in 63 Brook Street in 1896, and this became his private surgery as well.

Lizzie Hughes has been an extraordinary absence in John Williams's archive. Of course it could be argued that she kept her papers and effects separate from his, but if that was the case, who would be holding them, and why? Much more likely is that John Williams – or his mother-in-law, who outlived them both – destroyed Lizzie's effects after her death, removing what must have been a record of something that they would all rather pretend had never happened. We know Lizzie kept a diary early on in their marriage; perhaps she kept one throughout their time together but it was destroyed by her husband when she was no longer there to keep it safe? We know from the defaced copy of his 1888 diary that he kept things, even when rendered useless – why not hers? Maybe she wrote about things that he would rather not let posterity know about. His affair with Mary, for example.

Among the few effects of Lizzie's in his archive are a large stack of postcards, sent to her in the last years of her life. Mostly these are addressed to Lady Williams, with but a few sent to 'Sir John'. None of these was of any direct interest but they did show us that Lizzie was warmly loved by her friends, and they remembered her and wrote to her often. Some of her correspondents simply mention that the card could be added to her 'collection'; others, a small poignant handful, express deep affection for her. Unlike her husband, who could only raise admiration in his peers, she was obviously capable of inspiring deep affection.

In 1903 John Williams retired from private work and moved to the coast beyond Swansea, to the village of Llanstephan. This village nestled in its own little cove while on the hill behind it sat a castle, and the 'magnificent mansion', as the local guidebook calls it, of Plas Llanstephan, which is where 'Royal Surgeon' (also from the guidebook) Sir John and Lady Williams lived. It was in Llanstephan that the flowering of his wealth and power showed itself, while Aberystwyth represented his twilight years, with the great achievement of the National Library of Wales behind him. He was a presence within the village, chairing parish council meetings to discuss important issues such as the sobriety, or otherwise, of the ferryman who worked out of the little harbour, or the matter of lighting in the village – a vexed issue that culminated with one meeting ending 'in disorder'.

Life in Plas Llanstephan must have been delightful. It was a large house, unchanged – at least externally – from the time that Sir John and his wife lived there through to the present day. The house, built in the second half of the sixteenth century and enlarged and rebuilt in the 1780s, is an imposing white mansion that sits on the hillside above the village overlooking the old castle on the opposite hill. It commands impressive views over the Towy estuary.

Such a large house seems a world away from the small farmhouse at Blaen Llynant, a powerful symbol of just how far he had come in life. Four servants, all women in their twenties, none of them from Wales, lived alongside Sir John and Lady Williams in the large mansion. In such a rural location, and set apart from the village, it must have seemed the perfect retreat for the doctor and his family. He was clearly putting all his London affairs gradually behind him, so much so that in one of the obituaries published many years after his death, the writer remarked that 'so renowned was his association with the National Library of Wales, that many men and women forgot the pioneering gynaecologist of the 1870s.'

From Plas Llanstephan, Sir John travelled up to London regularly for the General Medical Council meetings although he had retired from all active duties in medicine, both public and private, but his life in London was over, and it was to this beautiful house that he would happily return. Here too he built up his large collections of Welsh manuscripts and printed books, adding to the already substantial collection he had started in London. In the bibliographic records of the National Library, the bulk of these documents are referred to as 'the Llanstephan manuscripts', from where they were shipped up to Aberystwyth when the library was established. Here, at his rural home, he held the meetings with those who were also involved in the founding of the National Library – John Humphreys Davies, Dr Gwenogvyrn Evans and others.

The site of the National Library was an enormous issue in Wales, but Sir John would tolerate no opposition to his choice of Aberystwyth for its home. It helped that the land on which the library sat had been donated to the cause. His trump card against any arguments put forward by prominent citizens in Cardiff or Swansea was that he simply refused to send his collection anywhere but Aberystwyth. If the National Library was not there, he would simply send his collection, the finest in Wales, to the University Library in the town instead. His reasoning was a mixture of practicality and snobbery: Cardiff and Swansea would not do, because the readers at the library must have cheap living in the town available to them when they came to use the library's facilities. It must be somewhere where the casual passer-by would not drop in to read the newspaper and fall asleep in an armchair; and it must not be somewhere where tourists would just tick it off their list of sights to see. More tellingly, he did not think that Cardiff's 'mongrel and non-Welsh population' (as he wrote in a letter to J.H. Davies) would be the right people to look after his precious books and papers. The ill temper that characterised the debate over the home of the library culminated in editorials in the *Western Mail,* with statements such as 'it is Wales's misfortune that she cannot possess that library in the real sense of useful possession. At best it can only be hidden away in Aberystwyth,' or the council meetings reported that same day that accused Sir John of 'piracy' and his 'open antagonism to Cardiff'.

Aberystwyth is right in the middle of Wales's rugged coastline, and hugs the side of the bay that sweeps from the mountainous headland, with the electric cliff railway that runs up it, around to the castle that Owain Glyndwr occupied and which prompted the first use of cannon in Britain, as Prince Henry – later Henry V – sought to dislodge him.

Nowadays it has the same aspect as many of Britain's forgotten seaside towns; shabby, a poor mixture of large houses, peeling paint and the kind of attractions that seem only off-putting. Walking the streets in the evening, you can look out across the promenade to dark shingle and sharp ribbons of rock slicing into Cardigan Bay. The sound of the waves lapping the shore would have been audible to John Williams in his house, standing in the smart part of Marine Parade. He would not have recognised much more of the town, though; the barman in the hotel where we stayed maintained that the town had changed out of all recognition in the previous five years or so with the influx of students attending the college. Aberystwyth is a college town now, and you can see students on the beach playing football, setting up barbecues, smoking joints as they walk the streets, heading towards bars for cheap drink.

One such bar is the pub that now occupies the building, Blaen Llynant, named after his former family home, where John Williams lived for the last years of his life. The building, left by

John Williams to the National Library of Wales, now caters for throngs of students, and there is nothing left to be seen of the grand house and its equally grand occupants. We wandered up the stairs, peeped into the rooms (it's now a B&B), stood at the bar, and had a hurried drink. There was something ironic about this proud man's home having been turned into such a place.

John Williams lived in Blaen Llynant with his wife, Lizzie, and with his mother-in-law, from 1910, once he had put his heart and soul into making the National Library more of a reality than a dream. With his three servants, this would have been quite a household, and the imposing house on the seafront would have been busy with callers and with business being attended to at all times of the day. Once he stepped outside, the retired doctor would have been able to look down the sweep of Marine Parade to the headland where the castle sat, and dream of the independence that it represented. For Owain Glyndwr's stand here – and that of the defenders who resisted the Roundheads when they came to conquer the castle in the seventeenth century – was a rallying call for Welsh independence, a rallying call the doctor heard and tried to emulate in the symbol of Welsh culture and pride he was building on the hillside behind the town. In years to come the castle's mixed lineage, Welsh and English, would be represented in the combination of symbols stuck alongside it. The standing stones within the castle walls, known as the Gorsedd stones, were erected in 1915, for the National Eisteddfod, but were eclipsed by the tall war memorial raised after the First World War, bearing the names of those from the locality who had died in that conflict and the war that followed some twenty years later. By then, of course, John Williams had faced his own tragedy; his wife, Lizzie, died of cancer of the rectum, as her death certificate states, in 1915. He was left alone in his home with his mother-in-law.

Leaving his front door behind, the doctor would make his way down Marine Parade. Aberystwyth had become a popular town in the late Victorian age, with bathing machines on the beach and a water-powered cliff railway, a favourite of Victorian seaside towns, away to his right. On top of the hill was a Camera Obscura, where the image of the outside world was reflected down onto a table in a darkened room. In John Williams's time in the town, by now the Edwardian age, he would perhaps have gone by car to the library at the top of the hill away to the east of the town. We know he travelled frequently in cars, though he never owned one, from the numerous taxi bills that sit in his archive in the library. Perhaps he would stop first at a hotel for lunch; as one of the town's more important figures, he was often hosting meals there, both for the library and for the university. This impression of importance was largely created by the doctor himself, of course, and he even took the trouble to send out copies of his portrait to a hundred people or so – including the bank, for example – so that no one might have trouble recognising him. From everything we read, John Williams had become more difficult than ever; quick to criticise his peers, troublesome with those who disagreed with him, and harsh on those he considered beneath him.

Once Lizzie had died, the warmth must have seeped out of Blaen Llynant. In one of the short memorial pieces that appeared in the UCH magazine after his death, John Williams's old assistant, Herbert Spencer, recalled visiting the doctor, who complained not of missing his wife but of missing his work – work he had been in such a hurry to turn his back on in the early 1890s.

But there was still work to be done, when they first moved into the house on Marine Parade. The move from Plas Llanstephan in 1910 to Aberystwyth happened in time to oversee the building of the National Library. The building was begun with the blessing of John Williams's old friends, now King and Queen, George and Mary. The familiarity with which he had dealt with them in the past had now changed, and protocol demanded a different relationship with the Prince. Now the doctor had to write to the King's equerries, and every last detail of the King and Queen's trip to lay the foundation stones of the library had to be raised and queried, even down to the question of who was to be responsible for laying water on the road that the King and Queen would take from the railway station, so that the dust (should there be any) would not trouble them in their carriage. At this ceremony, the King also conferred upon Sir John Williams the honour of a Grand Cross of the Victorian Order – he had already received a Knight of the Victorian Order, in 1902.

A sad find in the archive was the invitation card for Lady Williams. Her invitation to the event, clearly marked 'Platform', did not allow her access to the Royal Pavilion where her husband was in attendance. But this distance between the couple was something that we started to see more often. It was most obvious in photographs, where she changed from the cheerful, smiling girl of the 1870s, still smartly dressed and fashionable in the 1880s, to growing thin, drawn, and unhappy. Her husband, meanwhile, took on a graver and more serious aspect as he grew older, and leaner, with a beard that made him seem even more stern.

Following his retirement, John Williams devoted the rest of his life to the National Library of Wales. The National Library was his long-held dream, and he was able to bring this to fruition through not only the political pressure he, and other prominent Welshmen could bring to bear on the government, but also through the vast collection of Welsh manuscripts and early printed materials which he had amassed over the years.

Sir John Williams died in May 1926. In his will, he left all his money to the National Library, and to the University in Aberystwyth, and nothing to his family. 'The library … will ever remain as the memorial of a far-seeing and single-minded man,' said the *Lancet*, in his obituary.

Chapter Nine

Whitechapel Road is a long street that runs all the way from the edge of the city of London, marked by the boundary of the Tower of London, up to Mile End, and the top of the Isle of Dogs. Today, buildings in shining glass rise in marvellous shapes, reaching for the sky in a way that makes this part of the city so dramatic – at least at one level. Down on ground level, however, where the people crowd together and the shops are crammed with cheap clothes, it is a different story. The smarter part of the city, Harley Street and Queen Anne Street, where Sir John lived and worked, is a world away from the cheapness and griminess of these East End streets. The houses in Harley Street are wide and tall, with grand porches and shining brass plates by the door that announce the names of the doctors (and there are many of them in each building), who work there. The streets are busy with traffic, but not many people walk along the broad pavements; and the shops sell nothing anyone wants or needs, just expensive things to clutter up their homes. The contrast with Whitechapel could hardly be more extreme.

Here in the East End is a part of London that has always been home to people moving to England for the first time. Now it is Somalis, before that Bangladeshis; in John Williams's time it had been Jews from eastern Europe. In the years before that French Huguenots, Protestants who were fleeing persecution in their homeland, had turned up here.

The names of the streets and other places there are familiar to anyone who has read about Jack the Ripper's crimes. A number of the roads have changed names since those times, some as a direct result of the association with Jack the Ripper, and others because buildings have been cleared and entire streets demolished to make way for new housing. Wartime bombs had done for many of the rest of the houses, and new ones had arisen in their place.

The Royal London Hospital looms over passers-by along Whitechapel High Road. The building is huge, and it must have been possible for a doctor to slip out, unnoticed, from a side door at night – and to return, perhaps with blood on his hands, and pass freely through its darkened corridors as he sought sanctuary. It makes sense, but would it really have been possible for someone to enter the building, unremarked, and unobserved? Is it also possible for a modern-day visitor to look further around the hospital and get a sense of what it must have been like at the time of the murders?

The Museum and Archive is listed on the notice board outside the hospital and located around the back of the building. The museum is based in an old crypt under the church at the centre of the hospital's grounds, down some small steps. Two rooms carry displays showing something of the history of the hospital. Despite the grand edifice on Whitechapel High Road, it is in this small room that history comes alive. The records of the hospital's inauguration, the tools with which it established itself; and the people that made its name – doctors, nurses, and patients – are kept behind glass. The history of the use of X-rays in diagnosis in hospitals, which, in the UK, started here; and the story of their nurse, Edith Cavell, shot by the Germans in 1915 for aiding the escape of wounded Allied soldiers, can also be found. There are some letters from Florence Nightingale, commemorating the long service given by the nurses in the institution. The largest case in the room is devoted to the most famous patient the hospital ever treated, Joseph Merrick, known as the Elephant Man, who had been found in 1888 by a doctor from the hospital in some local freak show and then brought to the hospital to live there. Society ladies came to visit the Elephant Man, their splendour contrasting with his grotesquely deformed head and body; so it was not unknown for smart people to travel from their grand houses in the centre of town to these grim streets in the east. If that was so, no one, either at home or in the hospital, would have been surprised by John Williams's visits. Unfortunately, John Williams was not registered as a doctor there. But the doctor had said in the letter to 'Morgan' that he was at a clinic here somewhere. It was just a case of being able to find out where.

The London Infirmary, as the institution was originally called, was established in 1740 in a house in Featherstone Street. It was soon apparent that converted houses were not adequate hospital buildings, and a new site at Whitechapel, the Mount and Mount Field, was purchased and building began in 1752. The London Hospital, as it was now known, partially opened in 1757. The building of the front block was completed in 1759. There have been many subsequent alterations, developments and extensions, but parts of the original building are still in use.

By the end of the nineteenth century, the London Hospital was the largest voluntary general hospital in the United Kingdom. In such a big place, maybe someone could work in a quiet, unnoticed way. In the early years of the twentieth century the number of beds passed one thousand on several occasions. The hospital was granted a royal title in 1990 and became known as the Royal London Hospital. Perhaps John Williams was a volunteer here, and that would explain why his name did not appear in the staff registers. He already worked at University College Hospital and maybe the rules of the time forbade him from working for another hospital as well.

Out on the streets of Whitechapel, although many changes have taken place, it is fairly easy to visit each murder site. The first woman to be killed was Mary Ann Nichols. Her body was found in Buck's Row, known now as Durward Street. It was a dingy street then, with small terraced houses backing onto yards. Now it is a typical modern London street; the old school at one end has been converted into a block of flats and the road is a procession of speed bumps.

It was early on the morning of Friday 31 August that Mary Ann Nichols's body was found. She was lying on the cobbled street, outside the entrance to a stable yard. Two workmen, making their way through the early dark morning to their jobs, came across the body, and, after feeling the coldness of her hands, realised that she must be dead. They went in search of a policeman but while they were away from the body, PC John Neil came across the woman. Unlike the two workmen, he was carrying a lantern and with its light he was able to see the slashed throat of the corpse and the blood oozing out of the wounds. Another policeman arrived and then the officer found by the two workmen came running towards them. He was despatched to fetch a doctor, Dr Llewellyn, of 152 Whitechapel Road, while PC Neil made enquiries in the buildings around the area to see if anyone had heard anything. The doctor arrived, and after checking the wounds in her throat, pronounced her dead. He felt not only her hands and wrists but also her legs, and the warmth in the latter led him to believe the woman had only been dead for some half an hour. As people were beginning to gather around the body, the doctor and the policemen decided it should be moved to the mortuary nearby. The body was picked up and placed on a cart, leaving behind, so Dr Llewellyn was later to state, 'not more than would fill two wine glasses' of blood.

It was only when the body was in the mortuary that Inspector Spratling made the awful discovery of the mutilations made to the woman's corpse. Her clothing was examined to see if she could be identified (her underclothing 'bore the mark' of Lambeth Workhouse and it was this that led the police, eventually, to her husband) and when they did so they noticed the terrible injuries to her abdomen.

Inspector Spratling noted down what Dr Llewellyn said as the doctor examined the body. The woman's throat had been cut, but the doctor noticed bruises on her right lower jaw and on her left cheek; 'the abdomen had been cut open from centre of bottom of ribs along [the] right side'; the stomach coating had been cut in several places, and there were two small stab wounds 'on private parts'. The doctor also noted that he thought the killer had been left-handed.

Mary Ann Nichols was a woman who had had a respectable life but lost it all to drink. Born Mary Ann (but more often known as Polly) Walker in 1845, she had married William Nichols in 1864 in St Bride's, Fleet Street, and settled down with him. Their marriage broke down at the end of the 1870s, and things declined swiftly after that. Her husband and children – they had five children, the youngest being ten when she died – had not seen her for three years before the murder, as she had made her way during the 1880s through a variety of workhouses and infirmaries in south-east and east London. In the final few months of her life, she had tried to better herself and had taken a job as a servant in the house of teetotallers, but this had failed and she had stolen from them before ending up in Flower and Dean Street, the most notorious street in Whitechapel, where she made her living as a prostitute and spent her earnings on drink.

The exact place where the woman's body was found can no longer be seen in Durward Street; where the old red brick of the school ends, and the new brick begins, is the site of the gateway where Mary Ann Nichols lay.

Annie Chapman was the second woman the Ripper killed, and this was perhaps the murder for which Uncle Jack had written his excuses to Morgan. Of all the victims, Annie Chapman stands out as a woman with little to live for. Sick with consumption, she was slowly dying; her husband had died some years before and her children were either dead or living abroad. She had been in a fight with another woman a few days before she died, and this had led her to visit the local infirmary for medicine. Perhaps she had seen John Williams? One of the male witnesses at her inquest stated that she had shown him some pills the night she had died, and told him that she had received them 'from the hospital'. Could these have come from the clinic where John Williams told his friend he was working?

At the inquest into her death, the coroner spoke about the dead woman's daily life:

> She lived principally in the common lodging houses in the neighbourhood of Spitalfields, where such as she herd like cattle, and she showed signs of great deprivation, as if she had been badly fed. The glimpses of life in these dens which the evidence in this case discloses is sufficient to make us feel that there is much in the nineteenth century civilisation of which we have small reason to be proud; but you [the jurymen] who are constantly called together to hear the sad tale of starvation, or semi-starvation, of misery, immorality, and wickedness which some of the occupants of the 5,000 beds in this district have every week to relate to coroner's inquests, do not require to be reminded of what life in a Spitalfields lodging-house means.

Chapman was a prostitute like Polly Nichols. What money she had she usually spent on drink, and when she tried to get her usual bed for the night on Saturday 8 September she was turned away for lack of her lodging money. Her body was discovered in the early hours of the following morning, in a yard behind Hanbury Street, still its name today.

This yard was commonly used by prostitutes and their clients from around the Whitechapel area, or so one witness, whose mother lived at number 29, told the inquest. On that Saturday morning, with the noise of the market opening nearby, John Davies left his rooms in number 29 at about 6 a.m., and immediately saw the body of a woman lying against the fence of number 27. As her skirts were raised to well above her groin, he quickly saw that she was not just another prostitute, sleeping off the drink, but that she was dead. He rushed out into the street to call for assistance from passers-by, and some of these men, on seeing the body, ran to find a policeman. They found Inspector Chandler, who called for Dr Phillips, the local divisional police surgeon. His testimony shows that the killer had taken more time with this victim – despite the fact that he had acted in a place where it was possible for him to be observed at any moment. While the doctor examined the body, the Inspector looked around the area and discovered that the victim's possessions had been removed from her pockets and placed beside the body – the inquest was told that they looked as if they had been 'arranged there'. The items included a portion of an envelope stamped 'London, Aug. 23, 1888' with the seal of the Royal Sussex Regiment on the back. In handwriting, the letters 'M' and, further down, 'Sp' were clearly visible. Inside the paper were two pills. (Later, the envelope was to prove a useless clue: it was a scrap of paper that Annie Chapman had picked up – in the house of the witness who testified to this at the inquest – to wrap around the pills, when she had dropped the box.) The Inspector also found, near a water tap and saturated with water, a leather apron.

Dr Phillips said after his examination of the corpse that the woman had probably been dead for two hours or longer. He also wrote that the woman's tongue was swollen and protruded between the teeth, which, he later told the inquest, would have happened if she had suffocated as a result of being 'partially strangled'. He went on, in his initial report: 'The small intestines and other portions were lying on the right side of the body on the ground above the right shoulder, but attached. There was a large quantity of blood, with a part of the stomach above the left shoulder.'

The body had also had items removed from it, specifically, 'the uterus and its appendages, with the upper portion of the vagina and the posterior two-thirds of the bladder'. The incisions 'were cleanly cut, avoiding the rectum, and dividing the vagina low enough to avoid injury to the *cervix uteri*. Obviously the work was that of an expert – of one, at least, who had such knowledge of anatomical or pathological examinations as to be enabled to secure the pelvic organs with one sweep of a knife.'

In his later statements, Dr Phillips expanded upon the idea that the killer was someone with expert knowledge. 'Anatomical knowledge was only less displayed or indicated in consequence of haste,' he said, and, 'the whole inference seems to me that the operation was performed to enable the perpetrator to obtain possession of these parts of the body.' The coroner agreed with him and went further: 'there were no meaningless cuts. It was done by one who knew where to find what he wanted, what difficulties he would have to contend against, and how he should use his knife, so as to abstract the organ without injury to it.'

Hanbury Street has not changed as much as Durward Street. Some of the houses around here are old enough to have been here when Annie walked this pavement looking for business. The brewery standing there now was on the site of 29 Hanbury Street, where her remains were discovered.

The double murder on the night of 30 September was one of the more extraordinary events in the Ripper's history. To have killed two women was in itself horrific, but to kill the second victim while the hue and cry over the first was still raging is extraordinary. Such coolness, such control at a time of great danger to himself, has always been noted by those who have written about the crimes. The two victims were, again, women in their forties who earned their money as best they could – sometimes this involved prostitution, sometimes not.

Liz Stride was Swedish, and was known as 'Long Liz'. She claimed to have lost her husband in an accident on the Thames, when two boats collided and between seven hundred and eight hundred people died. In fact, he died of heart disease in 1884, but her story made it easier for her to solicit money from sources such as, among others, the Swedish Church in London. She lived in and around Spitalfields, ending up in Flower and Dean Street, and earned money as a seamstress as well as an occasional prostitute. She, too, spent money on drink, and although she made appearances before the magistrates in her last few years for drunkenness, she was well liked by those who knew her, and regarded as a quiet and sober woman. But who would tell an inquest into the death of their friend anything different?

Catherine Eddowes, on the other hand, was arrested for drunkenness on Aldgate High Street on the evening before she died. She had been marching up and down the road impersonating a fire engine. She and her lover, John Kelly, had recently returned to London after spending some time in the fields of Kent, hop-picking. Eddowes had come to London as a young girl, but left when her parents died to work in Wolverhampton. She had stolen from her employers and run away to Birmingham where she met Thomas Conway. The two decided to live together; the initials 'TC' were tattooed in blue ink on Eddowes's forearm. Affection did not stop him, apparently, from beating her, and although they were together for twenty years she finally left him in 1881. Almost immediately after that she met John Kelly, and the two remained together until she died. Although she mainly used the name Conway mostly, it was Kelly's surname that she gave to the police when she was arrested for drunkenness. 'Mary Ann Kelly' was the woman they thought they had released that night.

The first of the night's victims, Liz Stride, was found in a narrow court just off Berner Street, underneath a socialist working men's club that was primarily used by the local Jewish community. On Saturday 29 September the hundred-strong meeting was addressed on the subject of 'why Jews should be Socialists'. When the meeting finished, between eleven thirty and midnight, those who stayed on chatted or sang in the upstairs rooms. At one in the morning, the steward of the club, a Russian Jew called Louis Diemschutz, came across the body of a woman on Berner Street between the club yard and the school opposite. He sought aid inside the club and the men went out into the streets, calling for the police, and PC Lamb, who had only recently passed the end of Berner Street, came to stand guard over the body while Dr Blackwell was sent for.

Dr Blackwell's examination of the body was the most exhaustive so far. It is obvious from the many accounts and interviews in the newspapers of the time that public interest in the killings was now at fever pitch. Dr Blackwell noted that the woman had had her scarf pulled very tightly around her throat, and that her face, neck, chest and legs were warm. He estimated that she had died within half an hour of his arrival.

Berner Street is now Henriques Street, a mixture of some older buildings, some open places, some bollards. The spot where Liz Stride's body was discovered is now a playground. Henriques Street has changed, but perhaps it is now what it had always been; a thoroughfare, nothing special.

But back in 1888, while the alarm was being raised in Berner Street, the Ripper moved swiftly westwards to kill Catherine Eddowes in Mitre Square. Mitre Square has changed, of course, with high-rise office buildings around it, but, as with Hanbury Street, it has retained its name. An effort has been made to brighten it up, with a raised bed of flowers, but not with much success. There is a suggestion – made in some of the more lurid walking guides – that people passing through here at night have 'seen' the ghost of Catherine Eddowes. Even standing there in daylight it seems an eerie, lonely place. A journalist at the time of the murders wrote that this square 'is as dull and lonely a spot as can be found anywhere in London'. So on a dark night in September, with all of the district in an uproar over the killings, this unfortunate woman was lured by a man into a grim place like this. She might have known him, certainly seemed to have trusted him – why else would she take such a risk?

The man who discovered her body was PC Watkins. He came through the square on his beat at 1.30 a.m., and saw nothing, but on returning at 1.44 a.m., he 'saw the body of a woman lying there on her back with her feet facing the square and her clothes up above her waist. I saw her throat was cut, her bowels protruding. The stomach was ripped up. She was lying in a pool of blood.' Inspector Collard was quickly notified and he arrived to find Dr Sequeira of 34 Jewry Street already on the scene. Although the doctor estimated that the woman had only been dead some fifteen minutes or so at that time (1.55 a.m.), he did not touch the body until Dr Frederick Brown arrived. The doctor noted that the corpse had been savagely mutilated; not only on her face, but also on her body, as the intestines had been removed from the abdominal cavity 'and placed over the right shoulder', with a portion cut away and placed between the body and the left arm. The autopsy would reveal that the killer had extracted both her left kidney and her womb, and that the mutilations had all been carried out after the woman's death – which in this case was caused by her throat being deeply severed. 'I should say that someone who knew the position of the kidney must have done it,' said the doctor at the inquest. Indeed, all the doctors who examined the body both at the murder site, and later at the City mortuary in Golden Lane agreed that the killer possessed medical knowledge – though they disagreed about the extent of his knowledge.

The murderer knew what he wanted and took it quickly – after all, the timetable from PC Watkins's beat showed that the killer took merely fifteen minutes to enter the square with his victim, kill her, and disembowel her, before making his escape – and at a time when he knew he might be caught at any moment. Perhaps the killer was equipped with more than enough medical knowledge – but did not have the time to make full use of it.

Following the killings, the murderer took away a portion of Catherine Eddowes's apron, soaked in blood, and discarded it outside 108-119 Goulston Street, the Wentworth Model Dwellings, where the words 'The Juwes are the men that will not be blamed for nothing' were chalked up on the wall. This has caused much controversy over the years, not least because the words were washed off the wall before they could be photographed, on the orders of the Sir Charles Warren, Chief

Commissioner of the Metropolitan Police. He did so, he said later, because he wanted to prevent any attacks on Jews that he thought the words might provoke. The building in Goulston Street still stands, though the archway where this infamous inscription was scrawled is now absorbed into the chip shop next door. Why had someone, whoever they were, written this line? Was it mischief-making? Or something designed to throw the police off his scent? Anti-Semitism was common in these days, and there is evidence that suggests the words of the Bible meant a lot to the killer. Perhaps, like many Christians then, he believed that the Jews were responsible for the death of Jesus Christ, and should in some way pay for this. Or perhaps, like some more recent commentators have suggested, the words were nothing to do with the murders at all. They were simply written up by an angry customer, who felt he had been badly served by one of the Jewish workmen in the area, and who had then gone on to excuse himself of any blame in the matter.

The last victim is of prime interest to modern readers because so much of her past has remained hidden all these years. Younger by far than any of the other women, the final victim was Mary Kelly, killed in her own home in 13 Miller's Court. Opposite where Annie Chapman had lived, and between numbers 26 and 27 Dorset Street, was an opening three foot wide that was the entrance to Miller's Court. There were six houses in the court, and the rooms were let by John McCarthy, who owned a chandler's shop at 27 Dorset Street.

The room where Mary Kelly died was approximately twelve feet square. Opposite the door was a fireplace. To the right of the door was a bedside table positioned so that the door would hit it when opened. Next to the table was a bed with the head against the door wall, its side against the right wall. The window closest to the door was broken and stuffed with rags, and Mary Kelly and her lover, Joe Barnett, would reach through the broken pane to release the spring lock of the door. Kelly's body was discovered lying on the bed, when Joe McCarthy sent

Thomas Bowyer along to collect rent long overdue. Bowyer looked through the window and saw the body – or what remained of it – in the room. He informed McCarthy, who, after seeing the mutilated remains for himself, ran to Commercial Road Police Station, from where he returned with Inspector Walter Beck. They were joined by Dr Thomas Bond whose notes (only recently rediscovered) give an insight into the awful fate of Mary Kelly.

> The whole of the surface of the abdomen and thighs was removed and the abdominal cavity emptied of its viscera. The breasts were cut off, the arms mutilated by several jagged wounds and the face hacked beyond recognition of the features. The tissues of the neck were severed all round down to the bone.
>
> Parts of Mary Kelly were found lying around the body; some, such as the heart, were missing.

Also found in the room by the police were remnants of clothes in the grate of the fireplace. They had been burned in a fire so hot that it melted the spout off a nearby kettle. It was assumed at the time that the missing parts of Mary Kelly's body were burnt in this fire, but there is some doubt about this.

For a while, Dorset Street became the most notorious site of the Ripper's crimes. Perhaps it was because she was killed in her room, rather than on the street, and the killer could take all the time he wanted. Perhaps it was because of her relative youth – Mary Kelly was in her twenties, and admired by many in the area as good-looking – that people were curious. Perhaps simply because the manner of the mutilations to her body after death were so vile. Visitors flocked to the site for some time after she died, but now there is nothing to see. The house where she died no longer exists; it was knocked down and is now a car park.

Chapter Ten

There were a number of institutions devoted to the care of the sick in the district, but John Williams may have set up a private clinic, and if he had done so it might be impossible to trace it due to the lack of records. In those days regulation was not what it is now; and the poor of Whitechapel were not protected then from the charlatans and others who would have preyed upon them. None of the books and articles about him mentioned Whitechapel at all.

The best record of a doctor's career, and the institutions in which he worked during that time, is in *The Medical Directory*. *The Medical Directory* is a fascinating and invaluable volume, recording particulars of registered doctors, and the institutions throughout the British Isles where they worked. These included both privately- and publicly-run institutions. Alongside the institutional entries, each doctor submitted an entry that gave their qualifications, their employment history and, if they wished, a list of their publications. There in black and white were John Williams's name, his address, where he had studied, which hospitals and other medical establishments he worked for, which societies he belonged to, and the papers he had written for various learned journals.

However, there was no mention, anywhere in the brief notes he made for the 1900 edition of the volume, that Dr Williams had worked in Whitechapel.

The entry listed Sir John's places of work as:

Royal Hospital for Women and Children
University College Hospital

St Pancras and Northern Dispensary
General Lying-In Hospital

It was apparent that John Williams, if nothing else, was a workaholic, for in addition to all this he also must have had a private practice. How could he possibly have found time on top of his other commitments to run a clinic in Whitechapel as well? The letter, in the doctor's own hand, which stated that he worked in Whitechapel, was starting to look as if it was impossible to verify. We had begun by thinking this was just a question of being able to find out where he had been based – and the official record was not going to be of any help. We had assumed because he had told us that he was in Whitechapel, we would find plenty of evidence to support that – but so far there was almost none.

The Medical Directory lists just one other in the Whitechapel section that deals with surgeons of the calibre of John Williams, and that is the Eastern Dispensary. The record that John Williams submitted to the *Directory* showed that he already worked in the St Pancras and Northern Dispensary close by to UCH; maybe he had a relationship with its sister institution in Whitechapel? If John Williams had used this dispensary as a clinic, then would this be a likely base for his nightly wanderings? Could he safely return to it from the streets and alleyways to escape the policemen, and the mob howling for the Ripper's blood?

The Eastern Dispensary still stands in Leman Street, close to all the murder sites, though it is now a pub. The building has not changed much since it was first constructed: the staircases are still made of stone, worn down from years of use, and the building feels as if it could be stripped of the modern additions – the bar, for instance – and returned to its previous state with ease.

Once more the elusiveness of John Williams prevailed after all these years; the records of the dispensary, which are kept at the Royal London Hospital, do not include anything about any official connection between this dispensary and the one in St

Pancras where we knew John Williams worked. Neither did the doctor's name appear in any of the records; nor was there any mention of any private clinics run on its premises.

The Eastern Dispensary was one of the many dispensaries set up in Victorian London as a product of Victorian philanthropy. Despite living in one of the richest nations on the earth, and in its proud capital, Victorians were acutely aware of the poverty within their own city. Whitechapel was the most appalling example of this, but throughout the city were pockets of poverty the equal of anything the Empire encompassed overseas. The influx of newcomers was hastened by the development and growth of large industries and the startling developments that the golden age of industry and science brought. The London of Sir John Williams had, recognisably, some of the features of London today: the Underground had opened, the streets were crowded with trams and buses (albeit horse-drawn ones), the telephone and the electric light had begun to appear in offices and houses throughout the capital. The metropolis had many the problems that we associate with it today – overcrowding, pollution, crime, poverty – and an infrastructure of social welfare had started to appear to deal with these.

Amidst this change and expansion, the medical world too kept pace. The chance of contracting an infection while in the care of the doctor and his assistants was now minimal, thanks to Sir Joseph Lister and the development of antiseptics, and abdominal operations could be more confidently carried out. Anaesthetics were administered routinely, and coming under the surgeon's knife was no longer the terrifying submission it had once been. Although the doctor was always male (the arrival of female doctors was not going to happen for some years, and women at that time were restricted to the ranks of midwives and nurses), nursing was now more professional, thanks to Florence Nightingale and her many co-workers. Once you had passed through the doctor's hands you were no longer at risk from a wayward nurse.

A Victorian doctor was not only stern and forbidding to most of his hospital patients, but he was also used to issuing orders and having them carried out – no need to jolly the patients along at the same time. There were many examples of this in the archives of John Williams, and they show just what a powerful position a doctor held then.

The entry for John Williams in *The Medical Directory* showed that one doctor could work at the same time in many different kinds of institutions in his career. Was the expectation from the people who worked there or were treated by him different at every one? Was there something special about the Eastern Dispensary, which meant that his name might not appear in the records – while at the same time it was clear that he had worked there?

John Williams had worked in all these different places at one time or another: public hospitals (University College, the Lying-In Hospital in Waterloo, the Hospital for Women and Children also in Waterloo), charitable dispensaries (the St Pancras and Northern Dispensary), private practice (his address was given as 11 Queen Anne Street), and various societies, the most important of which seemed to be the Society of Obstetricians and Gynaecologists.

A Victorian doctor worked in a hospital, preferably a big teaching hospital, in order to further his research and to pass on his knowledge. But it did not pay him well; the money he earned there was very little compared to what he could earn in private practice. However, it was in the big hospitals that he could research whatever specialisation he had chosen. Here he could develop a reputation, and so bring about the kind of increase in status that would allow him to expand his private practice, offer his expertise to more well-off patients, and ultimately charge more for his services. But he could not use his private patients for research; so he had to remain in the public hospitals in order to do this. The hospital needed the doctor, whose income came from his private work; the doctor needed the hospital, which helped give him the public reputation that his private work needed to flourish. They were mutually dependent.

There was, however, an additional strand of medicine a doctor was expected to practise. The Victorian love of philanthropy extended to medicine as much as to any other branch of life, and the surgeons in the hospitals were also expected to work in the dispensaries, which were smaller buildings that dealt with the same impoverished cases, only the patients did not need overnight accommodation. They were similar to a general practitioner's surgery, but staffed with about ten or so doctors, in the bigger dispensaries. The St Pancras and Northern Dispensary had, along with the general doctors on call, the services of dentists and, in the person of John Williams, a physician *accoucheur*, a doctor who specialised in assisting women through the difficulties of pregnancy, childbirth and related conditions. This particular dispensary was obviously connected to UCH in that the majority of the doctors who practised at the dispensary when required also worked at UCH. In 1854, the editors of the *Pictorial Handbook of London* wrote:

Dispensaries are by no means the least useful institutions
for the relief of the suffering poor. There are in London
and its immediate vicinity about 35 that may be classed
under the title of General Dispensaries, their purpose being
to relieve the sick, infirm, and lying-in at their own houses
or at the institutions. Some of these are 'provident' institutions; that is to say, the relief is not wholly charitable, but a
small weekly or periodical subscription is necessary to entitle a person to the benefits of attendance during a sickness.

There is a dislike among the metropolitan poor, and
indeed the English poor generally, to entering a hospital, so
that these dispensaries are of very great benefit, particularly
the provident institutions, as they have none of the humiliating effects which charitable relief produces on some
minds, while they encourage the domestic feelings and promote habits of economy and prudence ...

Most of the information we gathered about the St Pancras and Northern Dispensary comes from *The Medical Directory* for, in its Victorian way, it bureaucratically recorded every detail of the working life of institutions as well as doctors. So one can see at a glance when John Williams was on duty at the dispensary; and when he was able to see patients at UCH. It shows how busy the dispensary was, as the record also includes the number of patients that the dispensary's staff had treated over the year. And yet there was no mention of him at all at the Eastern Dispensary. It was not as well staffed as the St Pancras branch, although a physician *accoucheur*, Dr Henry Oldham, was listed. But there is no record of John Williams at all.

The archives that can be examined at the Royal London confirm that the Eastern Dispensary records contain no reference to John Williams running a temporary clinic there in the autumn of 1888. If a record had been found, it would have revealed the base he worked from. But the records do show something else, which hints at a link to John Williams.

It became apparent that to track down John Williams in East London we had to think about what was missing. For example, conversations that must have taken place without being noted down. Williams would not want people to know he had been working there – because working in Whitechapel would not enhance his status with private patients. So while he could not deny to Morgan that he was going to be in Whitechapel, he could conceal this information from the officious bodies of the Victorian medical establishment, who noted down everything that passed under their noses. It would be simple enough for him to explain to the people at the Eastern Dispensary; he did not want to harm his prospects in private practice, yet he wanted to explore something (he would have given them a good reason) in the female patients from the East End that did not present itself often enough in the treatment rooms in St Pancras, Waterloo, or Gower Street.

This becomes apparent when studying the detail of the history of the other doctor who *was* recorded as working at the dispensary. Dr Henry Oldham was listed as the *accoucheur* at the Eastern Dispensary. In his own entry in *The Medical Directory*, however, and when cross-referenced to another reference volume, *Munk's Roll*, or the *Lives of the Fellows of the Royal College of Surgeons*, it was clear that he had retired in 1882 and was living in Bournemouth. No matter what might be said about the efficiency of the railway system in the Victorian age, it seemed unlikely that a retired doctor would have travelled up from Bournemouth – at his own expense, too – on a regular basis to attend to the impoverished workers of Whitechapel.

The records showed that not only was Dr Oldham a member of the Society of Obstetricians and Gynaecologists, but that he also had a house in the street next to John Williams, when he had lived in London. It was possible that the two men knew each other well; and that, in an unofficial way, John Williams took over the duties that Dr Oldham could no longer perform. Furthermore, he asked for this not to be recorded in the files as he was simply doing an old friend a favour. The minutes of the management board of the Eastern Dispensary for 1891 record that 'it was felt that the [unnamed] *accoucheur* should be forced to attend on Tuesdays'. So this theory seemed likelier still. The doctor who had been doing that job had come and gone as he pleased. This would fit with what is known about the busy working life of John Williams, as he rushed between the various places where he practised. Also in the archive, in the minutes for February 1889, was the record that the board were pleased with the introduction of late opening hours on a Friday. The unnamed doctor who actually *did* the job that Dr Oldham had retired from would have had access to the building at the weekend – when each of the Ripper's victims was killed – and his lack of regular hours had annoyed the board enough that they insisted his replacement be made to work a specific day and time.

It is impossible that these two men – in the same field, in the same society, in the same part of London at the same time –

could not have known each other.

So would the archives at UCH strengthen the case for the Eastern Dispensary being John Williams's base in Whitechapel? The archives now sit in a special collections library in an unimpressive concrete block along an arterial route just north of the Euston Road. The materials held on Sir John Williams are easily located, as he was an important part of the hospital's obstetric department for over twenty years. Once again it was interesting to learn how the hospital was run and financed. In the days before the National Health Service, large teaching hospitals such as UCH were not state funded; they relied upon, among other sources of income, regular donations from well-off patrons to keep them in business. It was clear that no matter how prestigious UCH was, it had the same worries about money as the Eastern Dispensary's governors, noted in the records we had consulted the previous week.

It was the custom for the hospital's doctors to contribute towards the costs of the hospital, since their hospital work enhanced their earning power in private practice. John Williams, the accounts show, paid the sum of three guineas as an annual subscriber. Interestingly, however, he was not the only Williams who was paying an annual subscription to the hospital. Next to his name was that of his brother, Morgan Williams, who made the rather more generous donation of £50 a year, and next to them both, listed as a Life Governor, 'by special appointment', was Mrs John Williams.

Here was the first notice of Lizzie Williams having a hand in her husband's day-to-day life. Why had she been granted this title? In 1886, she had worked on a fund-raising committee for the hospital's fancy-dress ball, staged that summer, which, together with a bazaar, made a profit of £3217: a fabulous sum, when you think that an annual salary for a nurse at that time was probably around £15. Mrs Williams had worked on the committee with Mrs Graily Hewitt, the wife of her husband's superior in the hospital. What was that relationship like? Mrs

Williams came from Wales, so did Mrs Graily Hewitt patronise her as both a provincial girl and as the wife of the assistant to her husband? After this eventful summer, Mrs Williams made no further contribution to the records of the hospital's life, even though she remained a Life Governor.

John Williams worked as an obstetrician, under Dr Graily Hewitt, until 1887, when Graily Hewitt, who had worked at the hospital since 1865, retired. At the same meeting as Dr Graily Hewitt's resignation letter was read out, John Williams was appointed head of the department, and Dr Herbert Spencer became his assistant. The hours of attendance for Dr Williams were clearly specified: the Obstetric Physician would see in-patients on Mondays and Thursdays at 1.30 p.m., and out-patients at 2.00 p.m. on Wednesdays. Dr Spencer was expected to see additional out-patients on Tuesdays and Thursdays, also at 2.00 p.m. So it was evident that John Williams was free of all duties at the hospital on Fridays, allowing him to be elsewhere at the weekend.

Then something more interesting about his attendance times showed up. In 1889, the hours at which he saw in-patients changed; he continued to see women during the week, now on Tuesdays and Thursdays at 1.30 p.m., but he also added 9.00 a.m. on Saturday mornings to this list. Perhaps he wanted to make it difficult for himself to be elsewhere at those times; per-haps he wanted to have a ready excuse for no longer attending a voluntary clinic elsewhere. It seems a good explanation. His private practice had grown during his career, thanks no doubt to his appointment as physician *accoucheur* to Princess Beatrice, and at this stage he would have been expected to cut back on his working hours in the hospital, not to increase them. And yet he had done so, and *at the weekend* in particular; surely an even more concrete indication that this was a man who had used his weekends prior to 1889 for something that he did not want widely known.

Going back further in the minutes of the meetings of the hospital's medical committee reveals more of his working life there. John Williams had to list his annual holiday dates for the committee, and he took a long time off – usually two months over the summer – though, as this was not remarked upon in the notes, perhaps there was nothing unusual in this. In the meeting of 25 January 1888, John Williams told the committee that he had handed over to Dr Spencer all his teaching duties, as he now had 'care of beds' under his authority instead. It is probable that this was a managerial role requiring him to hold regular meetings at the hospital, presumably less onerous than standing in a lecture room in front of medical students. The minutes of the management committee through 1888 show that the hospital closed that summer 'for drainage alterations' for five weeks, so Dr Williams's holidays were extended that summer. In addition, the attendance notes for the committee show that John Williams was not present at any of the committee meetings that autumn until a meeting on 12 December, which he only attended in order to make a case for employing a third assistant in his department to deal with out-patients. In the following year, 1889, Williams attended every meeting, including one on 10 July, at which his request for new hours (involving him working on Saturday mornings) was approved. He continued to attend meetings far more regularly than he had in 1888, and at the end of the year was voted Dean of the Medical Committee.

At the end of the following year, in the meeting of 17 December 1890, John Williams told the committee that he wished to be 'relieved of the duty of performing ovariotomy'. He was relinquishing *exactly* the operation carried out by the Ripper on the streets of East London on the bodies of Annie Chapman and Catherine Eddowes, and which the murderer was assumed to have tried out – but had not had the time to complete – on the other victims, Polly Nichols and Liz Stride.

So within two years of the dates of the Ripper's crimes, John Williams had altered his working hours so as to tie himself down more to UCH, and to cease performing the operation that had made the Ripper such a notorious, and feared killer; two substantial leads linking him to the crimes.

One last record; in 1891, John Williams stepped down as Dean and did not appear on the minutes again until he announced his retirement. He did not appear to resign from the hospital in the same way as Dr Graily Hewitt – no letter was read out at the meeting, and although Dr Williams, like Dr Graily Hewitt, was appointed Consultant Obstetric Physician (with Dr Spencer promoted into his place), none of the usual courtesies in their addresses to the meeting from the other members of the committee were afforded to Dr Williams on his retirement.

The early and abrupt departure of John Williams from the place that had given him his first job in London, and where he had trained, was puzzling. The official history of University College Hospital, noted that, 'Williams retired from the active staff of UCH in 1893, having for some years in fact handed much of his work, including abdominal operations, to his successor Herbert Spencer.' It also said that Williams retired prematurely, on the grounds of ill health: John Williams retired at fifty-three, but during the remaining thirty-three years he managed to establish a national library – hardly the sign of a man who was suffering unduly from illness.

To summarise: John Williams had worked at UCH from 1872 through to 1893. During 1888, he had limited his hours to weekdays only, leaving the end of the week and the weekend free; only in 1889 did he reverse this and ask to work on a Saturday morning. He also sought to further reduce his workload at the hospital in 1888, giving up teaching; and in 1890 he had asked specifically to be relieved of the operation that had made the Ripper notorious. It seemed as if John Williams had worked at the Eastern Dispensary, covering for his friend Dr Oldham, and that he had ensured that he had the time away from UCH to carry out his work there. When he stopped working in Whitechapel, he put temptation behind him by making it impossible for him to leave UCH at the weekends, and then stopped carrying out the specific operation that was a reminder of his crimes. We felt sure that we had found the base from which Williams worked in Whitechapel – but we were wrong.

Chapter Eleven

Workhouses had existed since the Poor Law Amendment Act of 1834, which legislated for a Poor Law Commission in Whitehall, with local boards of Guardians responsible for each district overseeing them. In an area like Whitechapel, with so many people living on or below the poverty line, the workhouse would have played a crucial part in countless lives. Infirmaries were attached to all the large workhouses. Those who were too ill to work, and those who fell ill while in the workhouse, were taken there. The workhouse in Whitechapel was a huge institution, built on two sites to accommodate all those who had to live within its walls. The old site, in Baker's Row, was where the large infirmary stood five or six storeys high. Overnight, well over six hundred beds would be occupied. The new site, built in 1872, and south of Mile End Road, was the workhouse itself. Here over seven hundred impoverished people would be set demeaning and physically arduous tasks, but they would be fed, and given a warm and safe place to sleep at night.

Not only was Whitechapel probably the poorest district in London at that time, it was also a transitory place, where people travelled through without staying. The social commentator Charles Booth estimated that the number of middle-class people in Whitechapel in the late 1880s made up only 6 per cent of the population, which stood at about eighty thousand in total. The largest section of the remainder, by far, was the 'poor', whom he divided into sub-categories – poor, very poor, occasional labourers, and criminals. The numbers of 'poor' – with a man earning perhaps fifteen shillings a week – stood at 40 per cent of the population. It was known that there were more people in common boarding-houses in Whitechapel than anywhere else in England, and many of these were brothels – the police estimated there were over sixty of them in the district – for prostitution was, often, the only way for women to live. For many of them, including perhaps the Ripper's victims, it was an occasional occupation; they might earn a living by a variety of means, but in the end they all fell back on what came easiest.

The Whitechapel Infirmary in Baker's Row was part of an extensive network of buildings run by the Guardians under the Poor Law rules. In addition to the enormous infirmary, which housed over six hundred sick each night, there was also a workhouse, and the casual wards where the indigent poor could seek shelter. Close by were extensive buildings near the Mile End Road, known as the South Grove Workhouse. A contemporary account describes the place as if it were a gaol:

> a forecourt of neat flower beds, closely shaven grass plots, smooth paths, and trees which had been pruned until their branches had reached the legitimate amount of foliage. The Bastille stretched further than the eye could see, and seemed a standing rebuke to its poverty-stricken surroundings, for it was clean … not a spot on it, not a stain, nothing to show a trace of sympathy with the misery and sin of the people who lived in this neighbourhood.

The Clerk to the Governors at Whitechapel was William Vallance, and his influence can be felt to this day – Baker's Row is now known as Vallance Road. Vallance was an influential figure in the history of the Poor Law; even the Commissioners back in their palatial offices in Whitehall would consult him on matters of detail. The records that remain from his considerable efforts lie in archives in London, and in each volume of the archive one can find, painstakingly copied out in copperplate, examples of his work both with the Guardians whom he notionally served, and with the Commissioners in Whitehall with whom he corresponded.

In the records of a meeting at the Society of Obstetricians & Gynaecologists in 1881, a reference is made to a Dr J.J. Ilott. John Williams spoke in the presence of Dr Ilott, who joined the society in 1877, when John Williams was a member of the council. In 1881, Dr Ilott was working in Whitechapel, at the Workhouse Infirmary in Baker's Row, very near the London Hospital.

Was this our lead to John Williams's link with Whitechapel?

Looking at the 1891 map, the infirmary was tucked behind Whitechapel High Street, alongside some railway sidings, closer in fact to the murder sites than the Eastern Dispensary. However, we knew that John Williams had not noted anywhere in his records that he had worked there; and the records for the infirmary established that he had not been on the staff at any time. Would he necessarily want or need his work to be on record if it was voluntary? Especially if he would rather his private, and more importantly, wealthy patients did not find out about his connection with the notoriously impoverished and seedy East End district of London? Williams could have worked discreetly at the Whitechapel Workhouse Infirmary without listing it in any official record of his activities.

The archives for the Whitechapel Workhouse Infirmary lie in two separate depositories in London: in the modern building of the National Archives in Kew, which holds the correspondence between the Guardians and Whitehall, and official reports on the workhouse and its staff; and in the London Metropolitan Archives, a building in Clerkenwell housing hundreds of tons of documents from public institutions in the London area, including the day-to-day records of the infirmary and workhouse. The volumes that we wanted to look through varied in their condition. Some were preserved in stiffened papers, which sealed the documents against further decay. Others almost crumbled in our hands and deposited clouds of dust over us as we gingerly turned the pages. It was astonishing to think that these records

22nd September 1885

					Compensation
10	73	12	12	6	Rev G. Eastman
		18	.	.	A. M. Champneys
					Relieving Officers
18		4	.	.	J. C. McDonald
20		2	.	.	J. Eagles
					Steward
114		34	.	.	C.H. Simcock
		34	.	.	"
		34	.	.	"
					Master
117		25	.	.	S. Y. Walerer
					Invoice (Infirmary)
60		16	.	.	J. Westhop
		9	.	.	J. Williams
		26	6	.	G. A. Collier
					Lunatic
23		7	6	8	Bethnal Green
					Repairs &
81		62	1	.	G. A. Collier

13th December 1885					Rations
12 L	161	L	3	L	C. H. Limcock
					Superannuation
115		L	3	L	J. Mooby
		L	2	6	S. Beecroft
		22	10	.	M. Mayer
		5	15	.	C. Nickson
					Compensation
116		12	12	6	Rev. E. Cashman
					Relieving Officers
16		L	.	.	J. L. McDonald
18		6	.	.	J. Eagle
					Steward
119		34	.	.	C. H. Limcock
		34	.	.	"
		34	.	.	"
					Master
122		30	.	.	S. H. Walker
					Invoice
57		16	.	.	J. Westhorp
		9	.	.	J. Williams
					Rates, Taxes etc
100		137	18	.	E. N. Vignes

P. T. O.

In 1885, John Williams noted that he had treated Mary Ann Nichols. In the invoice book for the Infirmary of the Whitechapel Workhouse, in the September and December records of that year, John Williams is shown as being paid £9 for unspecified reasons linked to the infirmary. No John Williams listed in the Whitechapel directories did business with the infirmary. (Corporation of London, London Metropolitan Archives, St B.G./Wh/68.)

had survived over a hundred years, and two world wars, and so many had come through unscathed.

Our readings led us through many dense volumes, all in copperplate script, about the workhouse; staffing, visitors, minutes of meetings, complaints from residents, financial reports, investigations into the background of nurses employed in the infirmary – until at last, one snowy January day, among entries from April 1885 to March 1886, outlining payments to plumbers, decorators, tea merchants and so on, we came across two records of payments to J. Williams. We almost missed the entries, as we had been automatically searching for the title Doctor to appear before his name. But there it was, just plain J. Williams. We did not immediately get too excited. How could we be sure that this was John, and not James? And even then, how would we know it was the right John Williams?

Then we noticed, at the top of the same page, a payment made to A. Champneys. This, we knew, was the uncommon name belonging to one of the district medical officers for Whitechapel. Alexander Mundell Champneys was a doctor, yet the register did not record his title; so it was possible that 'J. Williams' was also a doctor. Then there was the question of the size of the payments. These totalled £18, a sum equivalent to the annual salary paid to one of the infirmary's nurses. An amount that size, if it was paid to one of the tradesmen dealing with the infirmary, was usually cleared by the Board in Whitehall; as there was no such clarification, it is unlikely to have been for anything other than medical services. To double check this, we looked through copies of *Kelly's Directories* which covered tradesmen in East London. There was no one named either John or James Williams in Whitechapel who did business with the infirmary.

If John Williams had indeed had this professional connection with Whitechapel, it went a long way to confirming what his letter to Morgan had indicated – that on at least one of the murder dates he had been in Whitechapel. Not only that, but also, through his link with the Workhouse Infirmary, he might have come into contact with women of all kinds within the district – including, possibly, all four of the remaining Ripper victims.

In his own handwriting, John Williams recorded that he had performed an abortion on Mary Ann Nichols in 1885; and 'J. Williams' was paid for unknown tasks in the autumn of 1885, at the Whitechapel Workhouse Infirmary. This was the first independent indication of John Williams's connection with Whitechapel, which, coupled with the letter in the doctor's own hand, made it seem as if a case was building against him.

Whitechapel was a place of fascination to many Victorians, many of whom were painfully aware of the extent of the poverty there, and, acting upon their religious and social convictions, tried to do something about it. For many others, it was a place where they could show the extent of their philanthropy, and visit the area to 'do good works', before returning to their comfortable homes in the sure knowledge they had just improved their chances of religious salvation. For others still, it was a playground, a place to shelve their morals, and to indulge their every whim.

Many 'missionaries' made their way to the East End to do something about the condition of the people there. Some were motivated by religion, such as the Reverend Billing, who, as well as being a member of the Board of Guardians of the Whitechapel Workhouse, was a familiar figure in the Victorian press at the time, venting his rage at the slow progress of change in living conditions. Others might be those with more political motivations, such as Clara Collet, one of the contributors to the magnificent work on the Victorian poor compiled by Charles Booth. She lived amongst the people she wrote about; her commitment was to understand, catalogue and publicise the dreadful lives of the women of the East End.

Miss Louisa Twining, who features in much of the literature about the Poor Laws and the management of the workhouses in London, devoted her time to the improvement of those less fortunate than her, but her standard of living was completely unaffected by those she sought to help. Margot Asquith recalled in her autobiography the months she spent in Whitechapel in the autumn of 1888, visiting some girls who worked in the Cliffords factory there (and went with her 'girls' to visit the place where Mary Kelly died: 'the girls and I visited what journalists called "the scene of the tragedy". It was strange watching crowds of people collected daily to see nothing but an archway.'). David Lloyd George also took it upon himself to visit Whitechapel in 1888, to 'see to the bottom of things', while clearly enjoying the *frisson* of seeing such degradation at first hand.

There were innumerable prostitutes and brothels, and many dark alleyways and side streets where the prostitutes could see to their customers if they could not afford a bed. The availability of flesh of all ages and of both sexes for the gratification of those with money was shocking to many visitors in those days, and firmly puts paid to the idea that Victorian London was a prim world of crinolined maidens and covered piano-legs. It was only in 1885 that the Criminal Law Amendment Act raised the age of consent for girls to sixteen; before then, prostitutes as young as twelve were commonplace on the streets of the East End. And this was a violent world, too; 'one of the greatest problems of the police in the bad old days,' recalled Walter Dew in his memoirs of his time as a detective in 'H' division, which covered Whitechapel, 'were organised gangs. Lawless characters banded together, and under some fancy name went about robbing and blackmailing honest tradesmen, assaulting innocent pedestrians, garrotting and fleecing drunken sailors, and preying upon the defenceless foreign element, chiefly poor Polish Jews.' Things were not really any better when the police were around, and, in Flower and Dean Street, where the majority of brothels and lodging-houses were, even the constables would only walk in pairs. 'A single constable would have been lucky to reach the other end unscathed,' wrote Dew.

Despite the best efforts of the officials and leading citizens of Whitechapel, the East End was regarded as no less corrupt than the rest of London. In 1888 a parliamentary committee enquired into allegations that the authorities in London – the Boards of Guardians, the Boards of Works, and the various parish vestries – were spending ratepayers' money to fight reform. Complaints against maltreatment by the Master of the Whitechapel Workhouse, Mr Thomas Babcock, were frequent, mirrored only by the routine nature of the rejection of any such complaint by the Board of Guardians and their seniors, the Local Government Board. It was only for the offence of fiddling the accounts or – as in the case of one assistant doctor – caustically rejecting the opinion of the Board, that an employee of the workhouse and infirmary need fear for his job.

Into this environment, the arrival of Jack the Ripper caused dramatic changes to the slums, their surroundings, and the people who lived there. Indeed, in the last few years it has even been suggested that the killer was motivated partly by the desire to provoke public indignation at the scale of the poverty and filth amongst the people who lived there. It takes but a glance at the photograph of the mutilated body of Mary Kelly to reject this notion.

The Whitechapel Infirmary is no longer there. When the Poor Law reforms were superseded by changes in the early twentieth century, the workhouse system ended and the infirmary was turned into St Peter's Hospital. The hospital was later badly damaged by bombing in the Second World War, and was therefore demolished rather than being transferred to the fledgling National Health Service.

William Vallance, an extraordinary mine of information about the workings of the Poor Law, was a stickler for detail and nowhere is this better illustrated than in the entry he made for the fortnightly meeting of the Board of Guardians for 25 December 1888, when he notes, 'There were no Guardians present; and entry of the fact is accordingly made pursuant to Article 32 of the Order of 24th July 1847.' It was Christmas Day, after all.

Vallance's work is recorded in the vast dusty volumes available at the London Metropolitan Archive, and in the form of submissions to his superiors at the Local Government Board at the National Archives in Kew. Photographs of the old infirmary, now demolished, are on various websites, as well as plans and elevations in books at the British Library. It was a forbidding-looking place: one designed not to inspire as a sanctuary but as a place to dread. Its layout from these plans and from the notes given at its meetings can be imagined and, most importantly, (from a note written by the Clerk in 1889) we learn that the 'existing mortuary and Post-Mortem Room is not within the curtilage of the Infirmary, but at a distance of some 300 yards therefrom'. This is important because it meant that whoever was in that room – presumably not one visited often – was effectively invisible at night to the infirmary officials, and that he or she could come and go as they pleased.

The workhouses were brought into being through the efforts of parliament; under the terms of the 1834 New Poor Law, they were designed to bring to an end the excesses of public spending on poverty in any given area of the country. The cost of establishing and building them was borne by the creation of unions of parishes, and their management was overseen by local guardians of the poor. Within twenty years of their taking over the care of the poor, the workhouse system was the largest civil organisation in the country, having seven hundred institutions. In order to receive assistance, however, poor people had to be overseen; they were to live in the workhouse, and they had to give up all their personal belongings and any effects that could be sold to pay for their upkeep. This meant of course the break-up of houses, and the separation of families. Called 'bastilles' by the poor, they efficiently imprisoned the sick, the unemployed, the disabled, the insane, and the elderly, all at a rate that made

The Victorian press had a field
day with the murders.

GHASTLY
MURDER
IN THE EAST-END.
DREADFUL MUTILATION OF A WOMAN.

Capture : Leather Apron

Another murder of a character even more diabolical than that perpetrated in Buck's Row, on Friday week, was discovered in the same neighbourhood, on Saturday morning. At about six o'clock a woman was found lying in a back yard at the foot of a passage leading into a lodging house in Old Brown's Lane, Spitalfields. The house is occupied by a Mrs. Richardson, who lets it out to lodgers, and the door which admits to this passage, at the foot of which lies the yard where the body was found, is always open for the convenience of lodgers. A lodger named Davis was going down to work at the time mentioned and found the woman lying on her back close to the flight of steps leading into the yard. Her throat was cut in a fearful manner. The woman's body had been completely ripped open, and the heart and other organs laying about the place, and portions of the entrails round the victim's neck. An excited crowd gathered in front of Mrs. Richardson's house and also round the mortuary in old Montague Street, whither the body was quickly conveyed. As the body lies in the rough coffin in which it has been placed in the mortuary—the same coffin in which the unfortunate Mrs. Nicholls was first placed—it presents a horrible sight. The body is that of a woman about 45 years of age. The height is exactly five feet. The complexion is fair, with wavy dark brown hair; the eyes are blue, and two lower teeth have been knocked out. The nose is rather large and prominent.

John Williams in the late 1880s around the time of the Whitechapel murders. The doctor, who was an enthusiast for 'hard work', was at the height of his physical powers.

The mansion at Plas Llanstephan, to which the Williamses retired in 1903.

Albert. Mary. Edward

W & D. Downey. *61, Ebury St SW.*

Henry.

George

JOHN.

The doctor brought many royal babies into the world, but he stayed in close touch with the children of King George V. The six children, including the 'Lost Prince', John, continued to send him Christmas cards and acknowledge his presents to them for many years.

Sir John Williams as an old man. The establishment of the National Library of Wales became all-consuming for him, while its site was a contentious issue for Welshmen. The *Western Mail* resented Sir John Williams's enthusiasm for Aberystwyth, and declared it should be built in Cardiff: 'At best it can only be hidden away in Aberystwyth.'

Sir John Williams visits the site at
Aberystwyth during the building of
the massive National Library. As
well as making a large financial
donation, he gave his vast book collection to the library, and became
its first President.

In the main reading room of the library,
Sir John Williams's statue sits high above
the readers. In his left hand, he holds the
plans for the library's construction.

A photo snatched at the National Library shows Tony Williams holding the knife found in Sir John Williams's collection. 'A strong knife, at least six inches long, very sharp, pointed at the top and about an inch in width,' said Dr Thomas Bond, who carried out autopsies on the victims of Jack the Ripper.

Also held in the collection are three glass slides, prepared for a microscope. 'No operation should be performed for cure simply, but also for investigation,' wrote the doctor.

The National Library of Wales, on a hill above Aberystwyth.

the taxpayer happy. The workhouses were the epitome of thrift and Victorian philanthropy.

Life within the workhouse infirmary was not happy. So many detested the workhouse it was inevitable that they sought to subvert its rules and regulations whenever they could, whatever the result. Maltreatment by those in authority who thought it their right to lord it over the poor was one problem; corruption and abuse were also rife. Bad behaviour was frequently marked out as requiring fierce punishment. Failure to do your 'work' – for example, chopping wood; unpicking jute – could result, if you were a young man, in three months' hard labour. Even to be fed was something of a privilege. With unrelenting efficiency, William Vallance laid out the dietary table made for the regular inhabitants of the infirmary:

Breakfast
5 oz bread
1/2 oz butter
1 pint tea

Dinner
4 oz cooked meat (5 times a week)
8 oz potato or other vegetable (5 times a week)
3 oz bread
  Once a week:
  14 oz suet pudding
  Irish stew
  Twice a week:
  Pea soup

Supper
4 oz bread
1/2 oz butter
1 pint tea

In the mid 1860s, the editor of the *Lancet* regarded the infirmaries of the workhouses as so disreputable in terms of the health and care they offered that he referred to them as 'antechambers of the grave'. Thanks to the efforts of one doctor, Dr Joseph Rogers, who stood up to the board of his infirmary, and who was determined to improve the reputation of the infirmaries, usually working against corrupt and bureaucratic boards, the infirmaries within the workhouses were gradually improved. The *British Medical Journal*, in its obituary of Dr Rogers in 1889, said of his efforts, 'Dr Rogers has turned over the stone of ancient abuse, and has shown the world ... the vermin that throve in the darkness. As might have been expected, there was a mighty squirming and wriggling.'

However, there was one thing that Rogers could not improve. The doctors who treated the patients were regarded by their medical peers as providing a second-class service. 'In the voluntary hospitals [such as University College Hospital], consultants were unpaid, but undertook the work for its prestige, its contact with wealthy patrons, and the fees from teaching. A workhouse doctor did not expect his work to increase his prestige, rather the reverse,' says A.J. Crowther in *The Workhouse System, 1834–1929*. When the Assistant Medical Officer of the infirmary, Dr David Whitfield, wanted to leave to take up another post, the Board – which was not known for generosity of spirit towards its employees – ensured that it was minuted that it was happy to see him go on to a better job, as the Board realised how tricky it was for a young medical man to do well in an infirmary; hardly encouraging for their other employees.

The Whitechapel Workhouse Infirmary was an enormous place. In 1889, Dr Herbert Larder, who replaced Dr Ilott as the Medical Officer of the Infirmary when Dr Ilott resigned in 1886, wrote to the Guardians about plans for enlarging the building. It was already treating over seven hundred residential patients every day, and for this there were ninety officers, including all the stokers, washerwomen, cooks, and scrubbers, as well as the medical staff, who numbered merely the medical officer, and his assistant, together with the nurses who worked on the wards. The medical staff in the infirmary were massively overworked, and they would have been only too happy to welcome a specialist into their midst who would relieve them of some of the work – particularly a specialist such as John Williams, who knew a lot about the conditions that so many of their women patients suffered from.

As we waded through the papers of the workhouse, two further clues revealed his presence in the infirmary. The first was the arrival of a nurse, Ellen Phillips, who had worked for the last four years at University College Hospital. UCH was a large institution (although *The Medical Directory* does not specify how many patients came through in any given year, the entry shows that it had the same large numbers of trained doctors as hospitals such as Guy's and the London, both of whom list over sixty thousand patients annually), and there would have been many nurses there; but, given John Williams's appointment 'In Charge of Beds', it is highly probable that she would have known him, at least enough to wish him good evening. Ellen Phillips was appointed in 1886, to the position of night nurse. Her character notice, sent to the Whitechapel Guardians by Sister Cecilia at UCH, says she 'was a good nurse and managed the wards and her patients well, but I was forced to dismiss her on account of her constant untruthfulness'. Despite this slur on her character, she was retained by the infirmary matron, who thought well of her, and her appointment was confirmed to the Local Government Board at the end of 1886 when the matron reported, through the ever-vigilant William Vallance, that Ellen Phillips was 'kind, attentive, patient, obedient and truthful as far as I can judge'. Ellen Phillips remained a night nurse until 11 June 1889 when she resigned. During her time at the infirmary, she was paid initially £18 a year, a sum rising to £22 about a year before she left (compared to the £18 paid to 'J. Williams' in the autumn of 1885).

Also interesting is the length of her stay – over two years – in the infirmary, at a time when the Board of Guardians was concerned about the turnover of nurses – particularly night nurses, whom they always found hard to attract to the job. When Deborah Gough, a night nurse, resigned in April 1888 after only a few months, she wrote that she was quitting her job because 'the matron does not wish the nurses to be at all comfortable.' She went on at some length about this, in a submission to the Guardians:

> I was left on a Block by myself for seven weeks and also
> for shorter periods with patients dying on each floor
> besides young babies to attend to and when a patient has
> died through the night I have been obliged to walk and get
> another patient to help me lay the body straight and put
> the large screens around the bed.

A compliant, familiar night nurse, grateful for her job, such as Ellen Phillips, would have been very glad of the knowledgeable assistance she received, from a doctor she knew to be eminently respectable. He would probably have remained too aloof to have been much company for her, but at least she would have been assured of some professional guidance and support during his late night visits. Perhaps this is why she stayed in the job for longer than Deborah Gough.

The second indication that John Williams might be working at the infirmary emerged in the events that followed Dr Ilott's resignation. Dr Ilott was forced to resign, in the summer of 1886, on account of what the Board of Guardians called his 'weakness of administration which is subversive of good order and management in the infirmary, even if not actually injurious in some cases to the patients'. The Infirmary Committee were shocked to discover that *all* the patients were on a supplementary diet, allowing them eggs and other indulgences. The committee were further shocked when, on being challenged about this expense, Dr Ilott simply took *all* the patients off this extra diet, waited a few days, then reintroduced it to the wards. When questioned about this by the Board of Guardians, he replied that he was endeavouring to ensure costs were properly cut, but he had to acknowledge that he was not up to the job and resigned, pleading long-term illness. He was granted a pension and retired.

He was not immediately replaced, and the discussions that followed his resignation may be the clue that John Williams was exerting an influence here. The Guardians, instead of appointing a new officer right away, chose to consider a proposal from the Clerk that the Medical Officer was not directly replaced, but instead his role be undertaken by 'a non-resident physician and a like surgeon with one or more resident assistants'. This was already the situation enjoyed by John Williams; the surgeon would arrive and be shown around by the assistant. The proposal was also seriously considered by the Local Government Board – who commissioned a special report, and Louisa Twining, only too well known to the Local Government Board on account of her longstanding work in aid of the poor, also recommended this approach. In a tract published in 1887 she outlined her case, first setting the scene: 'The Metropolitan Infirmaries alone contain no less than six thousand seven hundred inmates [overnight], and ten thousand deaths take place in them annually.'

She felt that the possibilities for research were wasted and that many of these deaths were preventable if only it were possible for someone to study the illnesses: 'I allude to the admission of additional medical men and medical students,' she went on, 'in order to give them the opportunities of studying those cases of chronic disease and decay which are rarely, if ever, found in our Hospitals on account of their long and tedious nature.' She cited the supportive comments of various doctors who were of the same opinion, including Timothy Homes, Surgeon at St Thomas's, who decried 'the mass of material for clinical instruction which is allowed to be wasted,' said one of them, Timothy Homes, Surgeon at St Thomas's.

The Local Government Board report outlined how the proposal would work:

> The visiting officers would receive a small honorarium for their services, say £100 each. But their principal inducement to serve would be the opportunity of studying chronic diseases which for want of room cannot be received into general hospitals and which, nevertheless, by the general admission of the medical profession, throughout Europe, are deserving of far more attention than can be given under the present circumstances to them. They would be accompanied by pupils.

We frequently puzzled over why Dr John Williams did not appear in the official records of the infirmary. We knew he was his own best champion, and that he liked to record every small detail of his working life in *The Medical Directory*. Then we realised why John Williams never officially announced that he was working at the Whitechapel Infirmary: he could not, because it was not lawful. However much the management of the infirmaries was leaning towards his, or Miss Twining's, proposal, and no matter that many of those whom he worked alongside clearly appreciated his experience and his abilities, it was still unlawful for a doctor to 'practise' upon the patients in a workhouse infirmary. The infirmaries were already changing; many now permitted visitors to come in and work there; 'lady visitors', presumably performing their charitable works and perhaps their religious missions at the same time, were there on a daily basis (so much so that they had regular meetings within the infirmary as a semi-official group) – so why not someone who could only bring benefits to the sick poor?

In the end, and with great reluctance, the Local Government Board acknowledged that they were powerless to effect this change; that it would require a change in the law, and, although they did not state this overtly, a change in the attitude of those unfortunates towards those who would treat them in the infirmaries.

Why was it illegal for doctors to work in these buildings, and why did society object to doctors researching in the workhouse infirmaries? Why was it impossible for someone like John Williams to work openly in the infirmary when they clearly needed him? In 1832, in an attempt to prevent corpses being stolen from graveyards, and then sold on to doctors for dissection, the government introduced the Anatomy Act. This stated that the bodies of those who died in the workhouses, which could not be taken for private burial by their families, would be offered to the anatomists and doctors. In 1882, 557 corpses from the London workhouses were supplied for dissection, with only 27 coming from the hospitals. (One writer estimated that there were 57,000 thousand bodies dissected in the hundred years that followed the introduction of the Anatomy Act; and that 'less than *half a per cent* came from anywhere other than institutions that housed the poor'.)

The workhouses were considered as a prison by the poor and the infirmaries were seen as worse. If you were unlucky enough to die there, your corpse would not even be granted the decency of a proper burial. You would end up on a table, your every private part exposed for all to see (dissections were still carried out in public, and were not yet closed to the curious and the morbid). Being poor was bad enough: being poor and dead meant you had no rights, not even to your own body. Hence, doctors were not welcomed into the infirmaries, and no teaching took place there. This view is confirmed in Ann Dally's history of surgery, *Women under the Knife*, in which she says: 'One might add that it has always been a tradition in medicine, and still is, though not so crudely, to experiment on poor or obscure patients and to use them for the benefit of rich or important patients.'

One further piece of circumstantial evidence came to the fore in this trawl through the London Metropolitan Archives. We had assumed that the note from John Williams to 'Morgan' saying he could not meet him (one of the original documents that had started this trail) was to John Williams's brother, and that Morgan Williams had returned from his home in the United States to visit his family – until, that is, we started to look in detail at the Whitechapel Workhouse Infirmary. In January 1885 – obviously a crucial year in the history of John Williams's relationship with Whitechapel, given that it was the year he recorded dealing with Mary Ann Nichols – another Morgan, Dr Morgan Davies, was appointed as Assistant Medical Officer to the Whitechapel Workhouse Infirmary. Formerly of the London Hospital, where he had been House Surgeon and Resident *accoucheur*, the same role as John Williams in his youth, Dr Davies was a difficult individual, as is shown in the arguments he had with many of his colleagues and superiors at the infirmary. A couple of months after joining the staff, Dr Davies was already causing trouble; Dr Ilott had to be called in by the Board to deal with a fracas between Dr Davies and the priest who tended to the religious well-being of the patients within the infirmary. A little later, Dr Davies was asked to resign.

He and Dr Ilott had purchased some medical instruments that they claimed were necessary for them to go about their business, but they neglected to get this cleared first through the parsimonious Guardians. When the Board heard of this, the equipment was sent back, as an unauthorised purchase. Dr Davies was livid, and ranted on (for several pages of his submissions to the Guardians and, because he wanted them to intervene in the dispute on his behalf, to the Local Government Board) about needing the freedom to work properly, with his knowledge being somewhat superior to theirs, and that he thought it was shocking to be overruled. When asked to apologise for bad language, he refused, the local government stepped in, and he was asked to resign. Dr Davies had been employed for just over eleven months; and Dr Ilott had to admit that the equipment had never even been removed from its packaging, so suggesting that the row had become an issue of Dr Davies's sense of self-impor-tance.

Dr Davies's ill-tempered letter made all sorts of accusations; some of them quite likely to be true, as we were able to confirm once we had looked through the memoirs of other workhouse doctors. But Dr Davies overstepped the mark with his abusive language. Quite why Dr Ilott let him send the letter, and did not deal with the Board himself, is in itself interesting (and may explain why Ilott was criticised for the way he ran the infirmary in the local government's report), but the Guardians never raised this issue.

What does this have to do with John Williams? Both he and Dr Davies were members of the same society – a London-based Welsh organisation, the Society of Cymmrodorion, designed to foster greater awareness of Welsh affairs, both cultural and political, in the capital – and they corresponded many times over the years. When Dr Davies retired after an undistinguished career (he never worked in a public hospital again and devoted the rest of his working life mainly to Welsh patients in the cap-ital), he retired to Aberystwyth, the same town as John Williams. He corresponded with John Williams until his death. Dr Davies was even rude about him in letters to other people, portraying Williams as unwilling to make the kinds of wider claims to Celtic inheritance that he himself would like to see in the National Library.

We came to believe it was therefore Morgan Davies, and not his brother, that John Williams was writing to in the early autumn of 1888. We had no evidence that Morgan Williams returned from America. The last notice we found of Morgan Williams is a copy of his will, lying in John Williams's archive in the National Library. Morgan died on 13 September 1918, and was buried in the graveyard of the Bethel Presbyterian Church in Harford, Maryland. He left a considerable sum, approaching $20,000, to his only surviving brother. Instead, here was a 'Morgan' who knew Williams and worked in the same institution that we believed John Williams used as his base in those awful months. This might also explain why Williams did not give any other reason for his presence in Whitechapel; if he should by chance meet Dr Davies in Whitechapel on that evening, better by far that he had told him that he was going to be there at the infirmary than try to conceal it. After all, John Williams had been visiting the place for years; who would suspect him?

So we know from his own hand that John Williams was working in Whitechapel, at least on an occasional basis. We know from his working schedules at UCH and elsewhere that he was only free from his duties in the hospitals and private practice at weekends; that he knew people who worked within the Whitechapel Infirmary and kept his role there private so as to protect the Board of Guardians from any legal complications related to his being there. We know that he used the research he gathered there to inform the papers he presented at the Society of Obstetricians and Gynaecologists and published in journals such as the *Lancet*; that one of his colleagues there had a long-standing working relationship with him, partly based on their shared Welsh inheritance; that the Board of Guardians had even considered, at one point, reorganising its medical staff so as to include someone exactly like him; that the post-mortem room, where he would be likely to carry out any dissections, was not within the infirmary itself but a short distance away. In sum, we had learned enough to believe that John Williams was a regular visitor to the Whitechapel Workhouse Infirmary.

Biographers and sketch writers are agreed about John Williams's published work: it did not amount to much. 'The list of his publications is not particularly impressive,' said Emyr Wyn Jones: 'John Williams's published works were not many,' said Iowerth Hughes Jones: 'Sir John was not a voluminous writer,' said his friend and colleague Herbert Spencer. For some years, Sir John published papers from talks at the Obstetrical Society; but, after 1888, apart from two lectures in the mid

1890s, published nothing further. During the 1880s, the papers show that he was concentrating his work on functions and diseases of the uterus. Here are some of the titles of his pieces:

The Structure of the Mucous Membrane of the Uterus and its Periodical Changes
(1874)

Growths in the Uterus
Tumours of the Ovary
Ovarian Inflammation
(1880)

The Pathology and Treatment of Membraneous Dysmenorrhoea
(1884)

The Natural History of Dysmenorrhoea
(1884)

The Corroding Ulcer of the Os Uterii, *with an account of the post-mortem findings*
(1885)

Involution of Puerperal Uterus in Absence of the Ovaries
(1885)

The Circulation of the Uterus, with its Physiological and Pathological Bearings
(1886)

Serious Perimetritis
(1885)

If, as we suspect, John Williams concentrated his work on what he felt might benefit himself most (not only in terms of his position within his peer group, but also with his own private research), these papers indicated his focus on specific diseases and problems. Did he suspect that his wife's infertility stemmed from a disease that he was familiar with? We have no clue to this; all we do know about her health is what is printed on her death certificate, that the cause of death was *carcinoma rectii* (cancer of the rectum).

The archives that we worked away in during the winter and spring months of 2003 were in marked contrast to the extraordinary things we were uncovering in the papers and journals they held. Grey, dull days sitting in the charmless 1960s room at the London Metropolitan Archives were enlivened only when it snowed. Each of the researchers – elderly men in their warm jumpers, worn over their shirts and ties, women in fleeces and thick glasses – wandered over to the window to gaze in wonder as the thick carpet of snow turned Clerkenwell into a canvas for children. A journey to the National Archives in Kew – a more modern building but with a large soulless reading room, at odds with its helpful staff – was interrupted by a lightning storm as we drove over Kew Bridge. Or the car park at the National Library in Aberystwyth; always packed to overflowing, with drivers circling, looking for empty spaces, ready to pounce when one came free, despite there being little sign of all these people once you were in the library itself. We tried to look as nonchalant as possible in these places; tried to look as if the information we were uncovering would not be of interest to anyone, when inwardly, at times, we were simultaneously horrified and enthralled when we found another link in the chain we were forming.

Chapter Twelve

Mary Kelly was the Ripper's final, and most enigmatic, victim. She was a young widow; and, according to her lover Joe Barnett, fairly quickly after her husband's death she became a prostitute. An Irish girl in Wales; a woman from the north in south Wales; a country girl once in London, perhaps even a working-class girl in the company of a rich man? It is not surprising that we cannot find much evidence of her life, only that of her death. She continues to exert a fascination on all those who study the Ripper's crimes because of two irrefutable facts: her youthfulness and attractiveness when compared to the other victims, and the terrible assault on her dead body.

We went about searching for information to corroborate the testimony of Joe Barnett given at the inquest on Mary Kelly's death. As it summarises the only known facts about her, it was the obvious place to begin. Although some of the facts were corroborated by a newspaper report published in the *Star* of 12 November 1888, a few days after her death, the *South Wales Daily News* of 14 November 1888 was unable to verify any of the details given in Joe Barnett's testimony. If it had proved so hard to check the facts when she had just died, it was going to be very hard for us today to get a clear picture of Mary Kelly's past.

No one has come close to finding out enough about her background to convince anyone that they had found the 'real' Mary. Some of the most famous theories have even suggested she was the reason why the Ripper killed in the first place. Why? Because she was different in almost every way from the other victims. She was younger, by some fifteen to twenty years, and she was prettier. Inspector Abberline, who headed the Ripper investigations, had been in Whitechapel's H Division for fourteen years. He would have known by sight many of the women in the area, and would have agreed with the view held by the police at the time that she was 'possessed of considerable personal charms'. She was a prostitute like the others, but the story of her life before, and her rapid fall from respectability to the slums of Whitechapel, was swifter and sadder as a result. She was also, unlike the other women, young and attractive enough to be able to leave this environment and change her life, as she had done before. She died in her own room. The other victims died in the street. Her body was appallingly dismembered and disfigured, more so than any of the other victims. This showed one crucial difference in the murders; the killer had allowed himself time with her, as he no longer had to cut her up quickly out on the street. Did he choose her as his final victim in part because he *could* take his time?

Joe Barnett's words at the inquest to the coroner were transcribed by the clerk to the court in language probably very different from that of Barnett, who was a porter at Billingsgate fish market. This is one reason to doubt the veracity of everything he is reported to have said.

> *She said she was born in Limerick, and went when very young to Wales. She did not say how long she lived there, but that she came to London about four years ago. Her father's name was John Kelly, a 'gaffer' or foreman in an iron works in Carnarvonshire, or Carmarthen. She said she had one sister, who was respectable, who travelled from market place to market place. This sister was very fond of her. There were six brothers living in London, and one was in the army. One of them was named Henry. I never saw the brothers to my knowledge. She said she was married when very young in Wales to a collier. I think the name was Davis or Davies. She said she had lived with him until*

he was killed in an explosion, but I cannot say how many
years since that was. Her age was, I believe, 16 when she
married. After her husband's death deceased went to
Cardiff to a cousin.

The Coroner:
Did she live there long?

Joe Barnett:
Yes, she was in an infirmary there for eight or nine months.
She was following a bad life with her cousin, who, as I
reckon, and as I often told her, was the cause of her down-
fall.

The Coroner:
After she left Cardiff did she come direct to London?

Joe Barnett:
Yes. She was in a gay house [a brothel] *in the West-end,*
but in what part she did not say. A gentleman came there
to her and asked her if she would like to go to France. She
said she did not like the part, but whether it was the part
or purpose I cannot say. She was not there more than a
fortnight, and she returned to England, and went to
Ratcliffe Highway.

Barnett then went on to give details about his first meeting with
Mary Kelly, and their life together. The report from the *Star*
mostly corroborates what Joe Barnett had to say, but there are
some additional details that are useful to note. It reported that
she called herself Marie Jeanette Kelly after her trip to Paris, and
some of the writers of the time follow this conceit. Returning to
her initial arrival in the East End, on Ratcliffe Highway, the
report continues:

Her father came from Wales, and tried to find her there; but, hearing from her companions that he was looking for her, Marie kept out of the way. A brother in the Second Battalion Scots Guards came to see her once, but beyond that she saw none of her relations, nor did she correspond with them. The authorities have been making inquiries concerning the soldier who, according to Barnett, was in the Second Battalion of the Scots Guards. That regiment is now in Dublin, and it is understood that inquiries will be immediately prosecuted there.

If there was a resolution to this inquiry, nothing has been recorded; nor is there any indication in the Home Office papers now in the National Archives that anyone was sought in Dublin in connection with Mary Kelly's death.

The *Star* report continues:

It has been stated more than once that Kelly was a native of Limerick, but a telegram received from that place last night says that inquiries made in that city have failed to identify the latest Whitechapel victim as a native of the town.

There is little doubt that Kelly came to London from Cardiff some five or six years ago, leaving in that town her friends, whom she has described as being well to do. She is stated to have been an excellent scholar and an artist.

It was best to take these reports – of Mary Kelly's talents with the brush, and her sobriety – with a pinch of salt; from reading all of the reports into the lives of the murdered women, as recalled by their friends and relatives at the inquests, it is clear that no one wanted to speak ill of the dead. All their good points were exaggerated, and their bad ones overlooked, but this made piecing together the truth about Mary Kelly's past that little bit harder. The *Star* had more detail to print about Mary Kelly's first experiences of London:

It would appear that on her arrival in London she made the acquaintance of a French lady residing in the neighbourhood of Knightsbridge, who, she informed her friends, led her into the degraded life which has brought about her untimely end. She made no secret of the fact that while she was with this lady she drove about in a carriage, and made several journeys to the French capital, and in fact led the life of a lady. By some means, however, at present not exactly clear, she suddenly drifted into the East End.

Here, the area that Joe Barnett roughly identifies as the West End is named as Knightsbridge. We believed the report that Mary Kelly was installed in Cleveland Street, but even if this were incorrect, she would not have been a five-minute stroll from John Williams's work or his home, but only a little further off in the opposite direction. Knightsbridge, after all, would be only a ten-minute ride away, by Hackney carriage or horse-drawn omnibus. The remarks about her swiftly descending to the East End led us to assume that her 'supporter', the man providing her with the income to live in such luxury, suddenly withdrew his financial aid and she found herself hastened across town as a result. This also suggested to us that the man had sufficient influence to ensure that she was made to leave behind any opportunity of making money in the West End, so that he would not have to come across her again. Unless, of course, he chose to. This demonstration of his power might account for the fact that Mary Kelly never told Joe Barnett who her 'gentleman' was. She knew the risks if she were to identify him. The *Star* reports:

Her first experiences of the East End appear to have commenced with Mrs Buki, who resided in one of the thoroughfares off Ratcliffe Highway, now known as St George's Street. Both women went to the French lady's residence, and demanded Kelly's box, which contained numerous costly dresses. From Mrs Buki's place, Kelly went to lodge with Mrs Carthy, at Breezer's Hill, Pennington Street. This place she left about 18 months or two years ago, and took up her quarters in Dorset Street. As to her ever having a child, the testimony is conflicting. Mrs Carthy declares positively that she never had one. Mrs Carthy states that the deceased when she left her place went to live with a man who was apparently in the building trade, and who she (Mrs Carthy) believed would have married her.

It appears from inquiries made at Carmarthen and Swansea, that after leaving the former place for the latter, Kelly, who was then only 17 years of age, entered the service of a Mrs Rees, who stands committed to the next assizes on a charge of procuring abortion, and who is the daughter of a medical man formerly resident at Carmarthen.

This last, intriguing line seems to be nothing more than a red herring in the report, but the connection with the 'medical man' is of interest. Was it the product of an overactive imagination, either on the part of the journalist or the person he spoke to? Or did Mary Kelly have to provide some kind of cover story one day to Joe Barnett, when she let slip that there was indeed 'a medical man' – a doctor who had come from the valleys of Carmarthen – in her past?

We needed to check the birth dates and the other facts of Mary Kelly's life mentioned in the sources. To do this, the most immediate resource is the 1881 census, a copy of which is readily available on CD-Rom, available from the Church of Jesus Christ of the Latter-Day Saints in Utah – better known as the Mormons. The Mormons have been busy transcribing the census into their computers over the last few years. They believe that marriages are binding not only on earth but also 'through all eternity'. They have begun to collect records from across Great Britain and Scandinavia so that members of the Church may have their deceased ancestors baptised, and thus see them in the afterlife. The compilation not just of the census records, but also of the birth, death and marriage records of Britain, makes their electronic record one of the most comprehensive genealogical resources available.

The data had been collected orally, as there were high levels of illiteracy in Britain at that time. (Mary Kelly was illiterate and used to ask Joe Barnett to read to her from the newspaper.) The census-takers recorded the information by hand, and it remained in that form until transcribed many years later by the Mormons. The census was taken then, as now, every ten years and so could not only identify people in their homes but also show in later years how life had changed for them; how many children joined the household, who within the family died, and exactly how many servants they may – or may not – have had. Like *The Medical Directory*, the census records were to prove invaluable to us.

The records for Swansea showed that there was a John Kelly living in the city in 1881 – although he did not have a daughter called Mary living with him. We knew from the estimates of her age when she died, twenty-three to twenty-five, that she would have been around fifteen or sixteen during the census of 1881. It was a disappointment that we could not find her on the sheets that identified 'John Kelly', born in Ireland but living in Swansea, and we seemed to have reached a dead end. But when a breakthrough came some weeks later it was in answer to a different question and from an unexpected source.

If a connection between John Williams and Mary Kelly could be proved, their common Welsh background would probably provide the key. The census surveys for South Wales in 1881 were interesting but ultimately unhelpful. There were Kellys all right, even a Mary Kelly in Swansea of about the right age, but her marriage certificate clearly revealed it was not her. According to Barnett, Mary Kelly's large family included seven brothers, a sister, and a father named John employed as foreman in an ironworks in Carmarthen or Carnarvonshire. These and other details that Barnett gave, under the pressure of the coroner's inquest, were specific. For us to track her down, given the scepticism with which we felt it was right to treat the details that Barnett gave, was going to be difficult if not impossible.

The ironworks, however, provided another interesting angle. We knew that Richard Hughes, the father of John Williams's wife Elizabeth, was a wealthy entrepreneur with interests in mining, steel, tin and iron. One of his factories was the Landore Tin Plate Works near Swansea. Could there be a connection between the Hughes family and Mary Kelly's father John, in his role as foreman of a South Wales ironworks? Much has been written about the industrial heritage of South Wales, but it was just our luck that the employment records of the Landore Tinplate Works had been lost. If the Kelly family were involved in the business – if the father was foreman of the works – then the proud Richard Hughes would have presented his new son-in-law to his key workers. Perhaps the son-in-law would be shown round the works and thereby meet Mary, the foreman's young daughter?

All we could find by way of an archive to the business was the following information. It was started in 1851, and Richard Hughes had as partners Messrs W. Thomas, John Powell and G.L. Morris. We knew that Hughes and Powell actually managed the place, so we could be sure that if Mary Kelly's father had worked there, he would be well known to John Williams's father-in-law. We also knew that the company ceased trading as the Landore Tinplate Company in 1897 and that it was then transferred to someone else – from such brief notes as we could find, it seemed that it was the creditors who took it over. The works were then closed in 1906.

However, we were sure Mary Kelly's family had moved on long before that. We reasoned that she had left home when young to marry the colliery worker, Davies, and that when she had drifted into prostitution after his death she had effectively cut all her ties with her family. Perhaps they did not want to acknowledge her as their child once they had read about her dissolute life. Maybe they did not recognise the 'Marie Jeanette Kelly' that the papers wrote about. Maybe, after her father died in 1883, the family had returned to Ireland and never knew what became of her.

It was worth returning to the documents that gave details of John Williams's time in Wales. The chances that the doctor met Mary Kelly in London were too slim. Their paths might have crossed in Wales; in London, where she lived initially only a few minutes' walk from both his home and his place of work; or in Whitechapel, where she died. It would have to be in Wales, from everything we knew about her family history. He met her there, took her to London and to Paris with him, and then he abandoned her.

In her biography of John Williams, Ruth Evans quotes John Williams on the subject of the beauties of Wales. 'There is a charming anecdote referring to the doctor's love of his home country,' she writes. 'John Williams praised the Vale of Towy as the only one worthy of its name in Wales. Asked what he thought of the Vale of Teifi or the Vale of Clwyd, he said: "The Vale of Teifi is a mere glen – and as to the Vale of Clwyd, it isn't a vale, it's a plain."' 'Charming', or contemptuous?

Clwyd is in North Wales, a part of the country which we had never associated with John Williams. Yet for John Williams to have commented so vehemently on its landscape, he must at least have visited the area. If so, perhaps he had lived there or had had a practice there at some time? It was definitely worth investigating. The trail led to Denbigh near Llandudno in North Wales, the biggest town in the Vale of Clwyd, where the relevant records were centralised. There was no reference to John Williams in the 1881 census of the area, but under the name Kelly we saw something we had almost given up hope of finding. It was an astonishing discovery.

In the Broughton Colliery Cottages, of Brymbo in Denbigh in

North Wales, lived a Kelly family, headed not by John but by Hubert. Hubert and his wife Bridget had nine children – seven brothers and two daughters. Michael, John, Hubert, Patrick, Thomas and their sisters Mary and Elizabeth were all born in Ireland. Garrett and Timothy were born in Denbigh. Mary, whose occupation was described as 'servant', was seventeen years old.

'There were six brothers,' Joe Barnett had told the inquest, and a sister. The younger of the Kellys of Denbigh was one year old in 1881, his brother Thomas only four. Perhaps one of them died – a high rate of mortality in children was very common in those times. Was this the family of Mary Kelly? We thought it highly likely, especially when we took into account the likelihood of Joe Barnett's testimony based on conversations with Mary Kelly being many months before and only hazily recalled. Did John Williams make a slighting remark about the area precisely because she *had* lived there?

We looked on through the census records, not really knowing what to search for. We then tried the obvious things – such as, who were her neighbours? Opening that page on screen revealed a fascinating piece of information. There, also in the Broughton Cottages, and in the cottage next to the Kellys', lived a family called Davies, and in that family was a twenty-five-year-old colliery worker called Jonathan. Our persistence had led us to stumble on something no one, not even the most accomplished Ripperologist, had succeeded in finding – the true family background and origins of Jack the Ripper's final victim.

There was more evidence that we might have found the right family. The Brymbo Colliery had lead smelting works, blast furnaces, iron ore mines and a foundry. This makes it possible to corroborate more of Joe Barnett's statement: Mary Kelly's father may indeed have worked as 'a foreman in an ironworks', although he was called Hubert and it was his second son who was John.

Joe Barnett said that Mary Kelly had told him her family had lived in Carmarthenshire in the south, not in the north. However, he had gone on to tell the inquest that Davies had died in a pit accident while young; and so we searched for reports of accidents and deaths in collieries throughout that region. Then, in the *Western Mail* dated 23 February 1882, we found something that explained the apparent contradiction. A fatal accident at Cwmpark in the Rhondda Valley, halfway between Swansea and Cardiff and about fifteen or sixteen miles from each, had killed four 'sinkers'. One of the dead was listed in the report as 'Jonathan Davies, aged 26, Queen Street, Pentre, who leaves a widow and one child'.

Jonathan Davies worked at the colliery, and we believe that he and the pretty young girl next door married – or went away together as if man and wife – and moved south, perhaps to escape from families who were unhappy with their relationship. We believe that this is the Jonathan that Mary Kelly followed to South Wales, and who then died in an accident at the coal mine in Cwmpark.

In at least one report on Mary Kelly after her death, it was noted that 'it was thought there was a child' from her marriage. What we discovered in the *Western Mail* would seem to add substance to this supposition. The twenty-six-year-old Jonathan Davies in the same press report would have been twenty-five in 1881, and so match the Jonathan Davies of the Denbigh census record. Pentre, near Cwmpark in Carmarthenshire, is a Welsh word meaning 'village' so this means the couple were living near the mine. All the details suddenly came together. We know too from Barnett that Mary Kelly said she lived in Cardiff (about twenty miles from Pentre) after her husband was killed, and that she was ill, spending time in Cardiff Infirmary. It seems plausible that, after her husband's death, a young girl like Mary Kelly would have been consumed with grief at being left a young widow with a child, and that this, combined with poverty, contributed to her illness. Especially so if the two of them had run away from their families, and had, as a result, cut themselves off from the support that could have been offered to Mary at that time. Pentre's proximity to Cardiff may explain why Mary Kelly ended up there; Barnett told the inquest that Mary Kelly's eventual descent into prostitution was due to her being drawn into it by a cousin of hers living in the city.

Later on we also learned that Dr Andrew Davies, one of the doctors in the Swansea practice where John Williams started his medical career, lived next door to the infirmary in Cardiff. Is it possible that Williams was introduced to a girl who had recently been brought into the infirmary?

One more document in the archives at Aberystwyth had passed unnoticed by us before now. John Williams had kept some papers owned by a man called John Parry. Parry was a Denbighshire councillor and we found the formal call to a council meeting, together with minutes of the previous meeting. Next to it was a newspaper clipping from the local paper, referring to this same meeting on Thursday, 7 November 1889: an odd thing to keep, especially as there is nothing like this on the following document. The next item in the collection was also from Denbigh, but it was much earlier; the note covering the roles of governors and inspections of schools in the Denbigh area in 1880.

Was this a reminder to John Williams of the woman he had met, many years ago, that he kept beside him? Was it through John Parry, and his work, that he first came across the young girl Mary Kelly? Did he remember her – she was after all supposed to have been very pretty – and then see her by chance again in South Wales? Did he keep these 'souvenirs' because they were safe to hang on to? There seemed no other reason why these were in the library's collection. Mary Kelly, according to the census report, was seventeen in 1881, so she would have been old enough to have attracted the doctor's eye. 'A pretty, buxom girl,' said a policeman who recalled her. Maybe the doctor saw her in Denbigh; found her again in Cardiff, older, distressed, and available?

In Denbigh, we looked for the admission records to the local schools. These, sadly, cannot be found; the relevant years are not in the archives. The three schools in this particular area nearest to the Brymbo Colliery cottages in Tanyfron Road were Pentre Broughton (the earliest admission records they hold date from 1897), Brymbo School (where there are no records to cover the relevant dates), and Vron school (the nearest school to the cottages). On the census return for the Kelly family, the dates of birth suggested to us that Patrick, Elizabeth, Garrett, Thomas, and baby Timothy, Mary Kelly's younger brothers and sister, would all have attended the local school. By stating that Patrick, Elizabeth and Garrett were 'scholars', the census confirmed that they were at school, and, being poor, it would have been the nearest village school. What would have happened to Mary Kelly herself remained a mystery. As with her siblings, there are no records that she attended this school; perhaps she attended school in Ireland. We knew she was illiterate. Was her schooling interrupted by the family's removal to Wales?

There is another possibility. Depending upon the date of the family's move to Wales, she could have ended up in one of these local schools after all, which might mean she would have learned to read only Welsh. Without knowing the exact dates, we cannot answer this last question with any certainty. We can, however, estimate the date by looking at the dates and places of birth of her two immediate siblings, her younger sister Elizabeth and younger brother Garrett. Elizabeth, ten in 1881, was registered as born in Ireland; as Garrett was registered as having been born in Denbigh, and, in 1881, being seven years old, that would put the date of Mary Kelly and her family arriving in Wales as somewhere between 1871 and 1874. Four-year-old Thomas Kelly was born in Ireland, but it seemed improbable that the whole family had returned then. So it is only a possibility that she went to the local school for some time at least, though with the records missing we will never be sure.

But was this confirmation of another link with John Williams? Were any of these schools listed in the papers that we had seen in the National Library? We returned to Aberystwyth to check, but were to be disappointed. The school that John Williams had kept papers upon, the school connected with 'John Parry', was a boys' grammar school called Ruthin. The trail had run cold, apart from one last connection with Denbigh in the papers: a jotting in one of Williams's notebooks about the churches near St Asaph, a town close to Mary Kelly's family home in Brymbo.

Putting all this evidence together, we realised how it was that John Williams could have known Mary Kelly. We could place both of them together in the same area of the country; then in the same town or even hospital building, where they might have had the opportunity to meet; then in the same area of a large city. It represented a remarkable chain of circumstantial evidence – in Denbigh, in Cardiff, in the West End of London, Paris and maybe even in Whitechapel.

We decided to look closely again at Joe Barnett's statement to the inquest, and with the benefit of everything we had now uncovered, confirm or refute what he had said:

1) She said she was born in Limerick, and went when very young to Wales.
2) She came to London about four years ago.
3) Her father's name was John Kelly.
4) He was a gaffer, foreman, in an ironworks.
5) She said she had one sister ... and six brothers, one in the army.
6) One of them was named Henry.
7) She said she was married at sixteen to a collier, Davis or Davies.
8) She lived with him until he was killed in an explosion.
9) She went to Cardiff to a cousin.
10) She was in an infirmary for eight or nine months.

The first point was confirmed in the census report from Denbigh; Mary Kelly was aged seventeen here, in 1881, and it says her place of birth was Ireland. That would have made her about twenty or twenty-one when she went to London. If she is the right woman, she would have been about twenty-five when she was killed – which is what all the estimates of her age at the time suggest. In the census, her father's name is Hubert. One of the brothers – older than her by some seven years – is called John. Perhaps Joe Barnett mixed them up when telling his story? Hubert died at the end of 1883; perhaps John became head of the family then?

We paused when we came to point four on our list. It would have been better if we had been able to find out more about Richard Hughes's business interests, and to see if there was any kind of relationship between the Hughes family and the Kellys. Perhaps Hubert Kelly did work for Richard Hughes earlier in his life? After all, the census records of the children's birthplaces show they moved around. Perhaps he lost his job for some reason; maybe he was in an ironworks, part-owned by Richard Hughes, and maybe because of that connection there was a link even then between John Williams and Mary Kelly? Maybe they had lived in Swansea for a time and he was the family doctor?

We were both tempted by this idea but knew we would never find records of it; there were no records left of John Williams's time as a newly-qualified doctor in Swansea, and nothing that we could find of the Kelly family being in South Wales.

The next point was one we dealt with easily. We saw that the number of brothers and sisters matched up, except that there was one more brother than Mary Kelly mentioned; but we thought that with infant mortality rates being what they were in those days it was very likely that the youngest, Timothy, had died while still a baby. Of course it could well have been the eldest, Michael, who died in some colliery accident; that would make John the head of the family once his father Hubert had died, and so perhaps account for the fact that Joe Barnett had called her father 'John'. Mary's sister was the only other daughter in the family, as Joe Barnett had correctly recalled. Then there was point number six; no brother was called Henry but there was a boy called Hubert. Perhaps this was another error of Joe Barnett's? Or were we on the wrong track? We felt not, on balance, especially when we considered point number seven.

It would seem that the young Mary Kelly fell for the boy next door. Twenty-five-year-old Jonathan Davies, together with Daniel and Hannah, his parents, and an eighteen year-old sister, Louisa, were neighbours. This was compelling evidence of having found the right Mary Kelly. Jonathan Davies was killed in an accident in Cwmpark, in South Wales, near Cardiff, in February 1882. The record of the explosion came in the *Western Mail*; sadly, deaths in coal mines were all too frequent, and a few short days before Jonathan Davies died, there had been a terrible accident in a mine in the north of England with many hundreds killed and injured. So perhaps it is not surprising that so few records can be found of the accident at Cwmpark.

We did find the following notice, regarding the inquest into the deaths of the four men, in a later edition of the local paper, the *Swansea & Glamorgan Herald, and Neath Advertiser*. Dated 15 March, it read: 'A verdict of accidental death was returned at the inquest on the four men who were killed at the New Pit, Cwmpark, last month. The owners intend presenting £100 to each of the families of the men who lost their lives.' Was this money used by Mary Kelly to set up her child with another family? Did it instead go to his family – if the couple were not actually married, would the money have not gone to them instead? Was this the beginning of her downfall; leading to her illness and then on to her wastrel of a cousin?

This cousin intrigued not only us but other writers on Mary Kelly. We looked through all the records for this woman – police records of prostitutes caught in Cardiff, even looking for 'Kellys' in the old directories, in case she had an address listed – but we uncovered nothing. We drew a blank.

The only lead we had was a short note that we had come across in the *South Wales Echo,* saying that Ellen Kelly, aged twenty-five, was jailed for four months in February 1882 for 'keeping a house of ill-repute'. The address given is 21 Ruby Street in Roath.

We looked up the 1881 records and first consulted those for 21 Ruby Street. A twenty-three-year-old widow lived there with her child. We widened the search for 'twenty-four-year-old Ellen Kelly'. When the search was complete, we had four entries to go through. The first one seemed to be a possibility. Ellen Kelly lived with Thomas and their two children in Bedwelty, which was about twenty miles or so north of Cardiff. The most interesting thing about her, though, was that her husband's occupation was as a roller at an ironworks. Perhaps this was where the Joe Barnett story gets confused. Maybe Mary told him her and her cousin's story and some of the details were mixed up in his mind. It seemed possible – Bedwelty was also not that far from Cwmpark – but when we consulted the 1891 census, we saw that not only was Ellen still with Thomas but she had had another eight children. We considered the others on our list. The next two women lived too far from Cardiff, so we looked at the last one.

Ellen Kelly was living in Homfray Street, which no longer exists. Her parents were born in Ireland, making it possible that they were cousins to Hubert and his family; and Ellen was listed as a charwoman. We looked at the 1891 census and found no trace of her at all. We turned to the 1871 census and found her, age fourteen, in Homfray Street. She had two sisters, one older, and a brother younger than her; their father was called John and he listed his occupation as 'labourer'. So although it was not definite that this was the cousin who had contributed to Mary Kelly's downfall, it did seem possible. Perhaps she was already friends with the woman in Ruby Street – they were the same age – and the fact that Mary had spoken of a father 'John' to Joe Barnett suggested we were not far off from the truth.

But if Mary did become a prostitute, there is even less likelihood of there being a record of her in Cardiff. If we accept that as a poor illiterate Irish girl she was outside most official paperwork, being a prostitute puts her further still beyond record. Henry Mayhew's book, *London Labour and the London Poor*, dryly noted that 'a very singular fact in connection with the census is that there is not a single individual returned as a prostitute'.

It was unbelievably frustrating when the records were missing. We knew there must be something somewhere that might help us, but in some cases it had been lost and in others destroyed. We went to the place where the local records are kept, but the old admission books had been lost long ago. The only thing that turned up was a note in the census records of Dr Andrew Davies, the partner in the Swansea practice where John Williams started, who had retired as a surgeon but lived next door to the infirmary. We studied the census record, which showed that he lived in Newport Road with his wife, Emily, their eight children, and three servants. We wondered whether Mary Kelly had worked for him.

John Williams had been disparaging about the area Mary Kelly lived in, when there was no other reason for him to have even been there. He also had a close link to the infirmary she once came to in Cardiff. We believe the two met when she was in Cardiff, and that she subsequently became part of his life.

Chapter Thirteen

When the doctor and his young wife settled in London, the promise of a great future must have seemed to beckon to John Williams. He was married to a lively, outgoing girl whose musical accomplishments had made her the toast of her provincial circle. He had returned to the institution he had trained in, and he was at last recognised there as worthy of the position he held. His father-in-law, proud of his son-in-law and determined to provide the best for his beloved only daughter, the offspring of his first marriage, was more than willing to help locate and finance the best of medical London's prestige addresses for the new arrival in town. Finally in the job the doctor from Wales had craved, John Williams was able to join London's medical elite, becoming a member of important societies such as the Society of Obstetricians and Gynaecologists, which allowed him to broaden his professional and social horizons by making friends and connections with doctors in other hospitals around town. His self-professed love of hard work paid off, and the keen young man was soon despatched to dissect specimens brought to the society, and report back to its members, as well as be summoned to sit on the society's committees.

A doctor's professional life began in a rush to achieve something of a name for himself; without that, he could not attract people to his private practice, which is of course how John Williams expected to make a living. So it was important that he be known around town, that he have a reputation of the right kind, and that he be seen to fulfil all the important duties that he was asked to do. Even then, it was difficult for the young Welsh doctor. His wife was willing to aid him in his endeavours, agreeing to fund-raise with the wife of the man who had chosen *not* to hire Dr Williams, and presumably appearing at enough social functions to ensure that the doctor was seen as a stable married man.

But, even then, setting up in private practice was hard, as we know from his obituary in the *Lancet*. His colleagues believed him to be outstanding – but they were not the ones paying the bills. A sense of desperation, allied with his ambition and determination to succeed, must have driven John Williams. What would make him money? A reputation. And what would make his reputation? To succeed where no one else had succeeded; to establish himself as a pioneer in an age of pioneers. In his chosen field, obstetrics, he *had* to be bold and do something no one else had done. This was an era of great change; as Ann Dally wrote, for two thousand years nothing much changed in medicine. Then 'in less than half a century it became surgical and spectacular'. That was what Williams needed to do – something *spectacular*.

In the realm of obstetrics and gynaecology, no field was of greater fascination to the doctors of the day than the vexing issue of the ovaries and of fertility – of how precisely the organs functioned, and what could be done to alleviate the condition of sterility.

Using the principles established by his earlier teacher, Lister, John Williams made an astute move. Abdominal surgery was risky; there was a huge risk of infection once the stomach was opened. If he could use surgery to alleviate and cure some of the conditions that he saw regularly in his patients, and then use Lister's techniques to counteract the chance of infection from surgery – and, furthermore, if he could use these same techniques to bring down the levels of infection within hospital wards – then he would have achieved something that would make his name. This, then, became the doctor's plan. With immense confidence in his own abilities, he performed surgery on cases which no one else would have dared to risk, and he succeeded where others had not. His gift to obstetrics, wrote one of his biographers, was the use of the abdominal operation to cure certain gynaecological problems.

So much is clear from what we can read about John Williams's public life. But there remains one problem; this procedure requires practice, and you are not going to get much private work if you kill some of your patients. It was all very well working in a large public hospital, but even there the chances were high that you would be risking more than the life of your patient. You might be losing a reputation that you were trying so hard to build up. Far better to do what had been done for centuries now; that is, take time to practise your work, and on those who would not – could not – complain about it. After all, such patients were going to die anyway if you did nothing. John Williams was neither the first doctor to think this way, nor the last.

John Williams was already used to charitable work, and to work far removed from the private surgeries of Harley Street. Not only did he work with servants and other members of the working classes in the hospital, but he also dealt with the impoverished at the dispensary attached to the hospital. This was still a bit too close to home for him, however, and the man who had been brought up to enjoy a more robust way of life than those cosseted middle and upper classes in the West End was not afraid to spend time with the indigent poor of the East End. He was hardly alone in this; when his friend Dr Herman of the London Hospital gave a paper to the Obstetrical Society in October 1881, on the 'Relation of Antiflexion of the Uterus to Dysmenorrhoea', he had used a base of 110 women as his evidence; of these, 68 were East End prostitutes. These were women who could not get medical help except if it was offered to them; the best they could hope for would be a bed in the infirmary, where three hundred other women would compete for the attentions of one medical officer and his assistant, and that the supply of drugs had not been cancelled on cost grounds that month. Of course, they would be only too happy to comply with the wealthy, distinguished doctors who came along and offered them assistance, and the possibility of relief from their pain, even if it meant they had to put up with something awful. They had no prospect of any other kind of help. Into such a world, 'a hotbed of disease' with the 'moral atmosphere as tainted as the material,' wrote the *Pall Mall Gazette*, John Williams would have been welcomed with open arms.

Visits to the infirmaries of the East End workhouses by well-off people from the western side of the city were common. The Whitechapel Workhouse Infirmary has a visitor's book: alongside well-meaning ladies, there were the odd names of unexpected visitors, including officers from the army. Perhaps this was similar to the larger hospitals and asylums, which were open to curious members of the public for people to visit; the story of the visitors to Bedlam, the hospital for the insane, is well known, and maybe other hospitals and infirmaries were also on the tourists' route. What can be said for sure is that when well-off and important visitors such as John Williams came to the infirmary, they would have been welcomed.

Dr Ilott, whom he had met one evening at the Society of Obstetricians and Gynaecologists, introduced John Williams to the Infirmary. Dr Ilott had joined the society in the year that John Williams became Honorary Secretary of the society; there is no doubt the two men would have known each other in those circumstances. Both doctors, after all, would have joined the society for the same reason – advancement. This was an opportunity to meet like-minded men, discuss their working conditions, hear papers presented on the new kinds of treatment being practised in the capital, and occasionally welcome visitors from further afield or even abroad to discuss their work with them. Dr Ilott would have been particularly keen to associate with his fellow doctors; a medical man within the workhouse infirmaries did not expect his work to increase his prestige, rather the reverse. Perhaps when they first talked, Dr Ilott simply invited Dr Williams to come and visit, to see the condition of the women in his care, and asked for the benefit of his wisdom; perhaps he had a specific case in mind to discuss with the doctor. At some point, though, in the course of the weeks following their first meeting, John Williams took a carriage east to Whitechapel, and walked through the workhouse gates for the first time.

Was he risking much as a junior doctor in doing so? We can presume that he had begun to find his feet in terms of his work in private practice; the fact that he had enough surplus money to start buying up the books and manuscripts that were later to be housed in the National Library in Aberystwyth indicates this. We can guess that life under Dr Graily Hewitt at University College Hospital was still tricky, judging from the irascible way the doctor took issue with John Williams's papers at the society's meetings; and perhaps that meant that the research the young Welshman needed to carry out, in order to achieve the kind of breakthrough that would earn him his reputation, was hampered by the control exerted over him by Dr Graily Hewitt. So a trip to the East End, to visit pliant and willing patients, would have been welcome indeed.

We also know that things were not what the doctor would have wanted at home. We suspect that he thought his young wife would become pregnant quite quickly; and by the time they had been married for five years, with no sign of a child, he had begun to give up hope. Long before he turned to the women of Whitechapel for solutions to his wife's infertility problems, though, John Williams was still trying to resolve them with Lizzie. Married life was not yet the trial it became. In the early 1880s, not all his life was tied up with work, and he and his wife made great use of all the attractions the capital city had to offer. We know that he joined various clubs, and that he took generous summer holidays (the records in University College Hospital show that he habitually took all of August and September off work). In 1881, the pair of them went on a long holiday to the

West Indies, which made a huge impression upon them both. It certainly must have been quite an adventure; the West Indies was hardly yet on the tourist trail, and this was quite a brave thing for the two of them to undertake.

By why did they go so far away, and if they wanted to travel the world and see great things, why not visit his brother Morgan in America? John Williams was an honorary member of some medical societies there, which he had never had the opportunity to visit; while Morgan was at least in touch with his brother's career, contributing (as an annual subscriber) to UCH's funds. America would have been a great place for the two of them to visit, and it seems surprising that they chose to go to the West Indies instead. Was it her choice? After all, while on their honeymoon, years earlier, John Williams had made visits to hospitals in Europe; a cruise to the West Indies, on the other hand, gave him no scope for such trips. Or was it his choice – a much more likely scenario, considering the way their marriage usually ran? Here he became part of her life, rather than the other way round; and there would be no visits to hospitals. This would be a rest cure for her, if her apparent absence from much of his day-to-day life was because she had been ill. So maybe this gives us a small indication of their state of mind at the time of the trip; Lizzie was to receive her husband's full attention. After nine years of wedded life, there were no children, and maybe this trip to the West Indies was going to be their last chance – for her to recover her health, and for him an attempt to take his mind off his work and focus it on her in such a way that she became pregnant.

However, this trip to the West Indies didn't seem to make any difference, and, after their return, John Williams was back to work with the same extraordinary levels of energy and commitment. The doctor continued to establish his reputation in London, and to build up his private practice; he was beginning to make a name for himself within the circles he moved in. Things, at work at least, were going well.

It is likely, though, that John Williams sought something else from life, other than work, and perhaps his frustrations at home were carried on into his working life. He might have been a trial to some poor student; he might have been a dictator to some poor nurse. But these people had the right to go elsewhere, the right to complain about his behaviour. They might not stay in their positions, but at least they could get away from him. Not so his patients; an impoverished woman would have to put up with what the doctor said to her, about her, and what he did to her. One patient who came before him with stomach complaints was noted as being 'very dull at school'. If John Williams felt frustrated at home, perhaps he was able to vent some of that frustration at work. Or at least with some of the places he went to for work; the wealthy women living in the squares of Belgravia and Mayfair would not have to put up with the doctor's bad temper.

If the trip to the West Indies failed to produce the child they both wanted, then the idea must have been building up in his mind that maybe his great breakthrough might be to conquer the issue of infertility; and that perhaps the women of the East End, far removed from the kind of attention under which he was used to working, were the right source of material for him to investigate.

The President of the Society of Obstetricians and Gynaecologists, Dr J. Matthews Duncan, speaking in 1881 – the same year as the Williamses travelled to the West Indies – and transcribed in the minutes into the third person, said:

He was astonished to find a general consensus that sterility was not only curable but frequently cured, and in many conditions of abnormality or disease. Many eminent men doubted the reality of so-called cures of sterility, and regarded all such as mere lucky coincidences. It was only lately that he had become quite convinced that sterility was sometimes cured, and, while he had often heard of cases under many conditions, as flexion, stenosis, stricture etc, he was not convinced of the reality of any cures except in those cases of combined dysmenorrhoea and sterility discussed in Dr Godson's paper.

So in the later 1870s and early 1880s it was believed by some of John Williams's colleagues that a courageous doctor could overcome problems such as sterility. As the barriers around medicine fell, what could not be achieved, with a strong will, clear intellect, and determination? There were also several dozen women prepared to submit themselves to the knife of a doctor who would brook no dissent from his vision.

What would John Williams have seen when he first visited the infirmary? What would life in the workhouse have been like, not only for its patients and inmates but also for staff such as Dr Ilott? We can piece together from the records held at the London Metropolitan Archives, and at the National Archives, something of the conditions. We can add to this from the reports carried in the local newspapers of the time, and we can refer to memoirs from those who stayed in the institution, such as the American writer Jack London, to give us a more vivid and personal picture than we are shown by the official records.

I have found that it is not easy to get into the casual ward of the workhouse. I have made two attempts now, and I shall shortly make a third. The first time I started out at seven o'clock in the evening with four shillings in my pocket. Herein I committed two errors. In the first place, the applicant for admission to the casual ward must be destitute, and as he is subjected to a rigorous search, he must really be destitute; and fourpence, much less four shillings, is sufficient affluence to disqualify him. In the second place, I made the mistake of tardiness. Seven o'clock in the evening is too late in the day for a pauper to get a pauper's bed.

For the benefit of gently nurtured and innocent folk, let me explain what a casual ward is. It is a building where the homeless, bedless, penniless man, if he be lucky, may casually rest his weary bones, and then work like a navvy next day to pay for it.

The first thing that becomes clear is that this was a place run on strict Victorian ideals of charity; the poor were not to be too well looked after, or they might become complacent and rely on the workhouse to provide them with shelter and food. The accommodation that was offered to them was only to be sought out of necessity, and not because it was convenient or saved a relative some money. The records show that those who were able to pay for the upkeep of their elderly or sick relatives, yet who sent them to be cared for on the parish's bill, were tracked down and made to pay. Non-payment was always treated as a great crime, just as the fit and healthy young people who found it necessary to stay in the workhouse were punished severely if they neglected, or avoided carrying out, their work. There was no punishment meted out by the courts, but there was a moral undertone to all the actions carried out by the workhouse staff and the Guardians who ran the place. This is not to say that they themselves always acted well; apart from the corruption that seemed endemic within certain unions, as the groups of parishes were called, they were very harsh. Poverty, for them, was a moral stain; and no unnecessary kindness was to be offered to those who were foolish enough to be afflicted by it.

Occasionally, one or other inmate would decide to complain – whether it be about the bullying, as they saw it, of an old woman, or the confiscation from an old man of his few possessions. Their complaints were inevitably aired by the Guardians, but almost always dismissed; these gentlemen wanted to be seen to be doing the right thing, but rarely issued reprimands to their staff for activities that appeared to be about keeping the poor in their place. Every month, a local government inspector would call and report on the numbers of patients and inmates within the workhouse walls; he would also record the names of those men and women who had been taken before the magistrate for misdemeanours such as neglecting their work.

A more personal view of a workhouse came from the pen of John Law, who wrote, in 1889:

> The Whitechapel Union is a model workhouse; that is to say it is the Poor Law incarnate in stone and brickwork. Doubtless this Bastille offers no premium to idle and improvident habits, but what shall we say of the woman, or man, maimed by misfortune, who must come there or die in the street?

Within this atmosphere, the autocratic, determined and well-to-do doctor from the West End of London would have fitted in very well indeed.

Charles Booth's pioneering work on the London poor, published in 1889, avoided criticism of the workhouse, but did include a map of the infirmary buildings. The large edifice of the institution on Baker's Row was backed with a building shaped like a capital 'H', with the final downstroke of the letter lying alongside the railway which ran down to Whitechapel Station on the main road. The main buildings stood six storeys high, while the lower-level workshops, storage buildings and mortuary stood further to the east, right up against the railway line. In October 1888 the Board of Guardians wrote to the residents of the houses alongside the private road running by the buildings on the side of the railway, saying that they, the Guardians, would fix and repair gates and locks, 'to keep the road free from nuisance'. Perhaps it was through these doors, leading onto open ground beside the railway line, that John Williams was able to pass without notice. Of course, he would not have seen this route when he first came to the workhouse; but where else would he have gone to, other than to the mortuary, to dissect the bodies of the women who had died in the infirmary in order to further his research? From this building he would have seen the unobserved route out into the dark alleyways and lanes of Whitechapel.

One other thing that we can see from the records is the nature of the buildings within the walls of the workhouse, and how it changed. Sometimes this was for simple reasons, such as the need to expand or improve facilities; sometimes for sad reasons, as when people died within the infirmary in a manner that required an inquest. Every time the local government inspector came to report on the infirmary, he would complain about the lack of a padded room in which lunatic patients could be safely restrained; every time he did so, the Board of Guardians replied that they did not have the space within the institution for such a room. Space was clearly at a premium, and the intermittent building works served to prevent the place from collapsing under the pressure of so many patients every night. Deaths within the institution were commonplace; but sometimes something out of the ordinary. In August 1887 Betsy Wilks, aged forty-nine, set herself alight with matches obtained from two boys who were looking over the wall into the yard. As a result of her suicide, the height of the external wall was raised by three feet. Most deaths were of course those of the elderly, but not always; many of the young children died, while forty-three-year-old 'book folder' Esther Shanley died in 1888 of rheumatism. In the April 1886 accounts, the cost of burials for the previous six month period is shown as £59 13 shillings and twopence.

One result of the new building works done during the course of the 1880s, and the subsequent expansion of some of the wards, was the lack of staff, and Dr Larder, who had replaced Dr Ilott when he decided to retire, was very concerned about this. He wrote that having twenty-two patients per nurse meant that the work is 'with difficulty carried on', and that staff absence due to illness or annual leave meant that 'we are in constant fear lest some unfortunate accident should occur'. This did not prevent him, as well as his assistant, from taking off the whole of August in 1888.

It became possible to see that, despite the amount of paper stored in the London Metropolitan Archive and the National Archives, there was an enormous amount of life going on at the infirmary that was not recorded. Who exactly were the 'lady visitors', and the 'mental teachers' who came in to work with some of the patients? How easy was it for someone to assume enough authority to enter the buildings freely, and would it be right to expect no record of their time within the walls at all?

It must have been clear to John Williams, even on his first visit, that he could do as he wished there. The need for him within the walls of the infirmary was probably greater than his need for those compliant patients. To begin with, his presence would have been entirely benign, at least in so far as his aim would have been to examine the women there. However, he would not have been there with their well-being in mind, but with the aim of satisfying his curiosity and exploring further his own particular interests. His interests did not stop at the walls of the infirmary. Nearby was the London Hospital where he would have seen Dr Herman, with whom of course he was linked not only through their association in the Obstetrical Society but also by a *Lancet* article in 1888 which talked of the triumvirate of Drs Williams and Herman and Champneys. We can also see this from firmer evidence; the records of the Lying-In Hospital in Waterloo (run by John Williams and Dr Champneys) show that Dr Herman was a subscriber to that institution. Clearly he had been persuaded to become so by his two friends, as he was not a subscriber to any other hospital, apart from his own. Finally, the two younger doctors contributed to John Williams's papers, read out at the Obstetrical Society; and were his secretaries when he was President. So, in Whitechapel, John Williams would have known not just Dr Ilott, but also Dr Herman, and he would have visited both regularly in his ongoing search to discover a medical process that would make his name, and his fortune.

There was one other link with Whitechapel that we established, and which may also point to John Williams being in the area. Once again, this came from the records of the Obstetrical Society, the records over which John Williams could exercise no control. In the 1880 volume of the *Transactions of the Obstetrical Society*, we learned of Dr George Roper, another fellow, who was a Physician to the Eastern Division of the Royal Maternity Charity, covering, among other areas, Whitechapel. Dr Roper lived in Queen Anne Street – as did John Williams – and worked at the Lying-In Hospital in Waterloo, where, of course, John Williams also worked.

In 1881, Dr Herman of the London Hospital mentioned that he had treated a patient previously seen by Dr Roper. Dr Roper added that she had also been seen by John Williams at the Lying-In Hospital in Waterloo. So this lets us know not only that the men knew each other, and that they discussed the patients that they shared; but also, crucially, that the patients moved about London. So the women that John Williams treated in Waterloo or even at UCH could well have been from other places, and this will be important when considering the evidence about Mary Ann Nichols.

We also know, from the records, that one of the victims of the double murder, Elizabeth Stride, killed by the Ripper on 30 September 1888, was resident in the Whitechapel Infirmary in 1881-2. Long before, John Williams had started working in the infirmary; and perhaps he had spoken to her and even examined her then. If that was the case, she was probably the first (of the five women killed in 1888) to have the misfortune to meet John Williams.

But it was not only the women patients in the infirmary that would feature later in John Williams's life; the most interesting person to work there is the Assistant Medical Officer, Dr Morgan Davies. We kept encountering his name, not only in the records of the infirmary and also in the National Library of Wales, but also in the books we consulted about the murders themselves. We believe that Dr Morgan Davies is a pivotal connection between John Williams and the infirmary, due to the evidence that he inadvertently supplies.

Dr Morgan Davies was born in 1851, and trained, just like John Williams, in Scotland – only not in Glasgow but in Aberdeen. He moved to London and qualified as a doctor at the London Hospital in Whitechapel, where he worked as a house physician, a house surgeon and, intriguingly, resident *accoucheur*. As far as it is possible to tell, he never joined the Society of Obstetricians, so it is unlikely that he rigorously pursued this later occupation with the same single-mindedness as Dr John Williams. He joined the staff of the Whitechapel Workhouse Infirmary, working as Dr Ilott's assistant, in January 1885, but this move could not be considered a step up in his career. Was Dr Davies also forced to leave the London Hospital as well as the infirmary because of his ill-judged attacks on his employers?

Shortly after Dr Davies joined the infirmary, he fell out with the chaplain. The meeting of 19 May 1885 had to deal with a 'misunderstanding' between the two men relating to the 'discharge of their respective duties in the wards of the infirmary'. It is hard to see how this could happen but Dr Davies succeeded in overstepping the mark.

Dr Davies never managed to get a job in a public hospital again, and he went on to live in and around the Whitechapel area for the rest of the century – in Kings Street, by Finsbury Square; in Goring Street, in Houndsditch; and for a while in Black Lyon Yard, Whitechapel (this latter address was the one he gave to the Honourable Society of Cymmrodorion, of which John Williams was a council member, a society devoted to the preservation and celebration of Welsh culture). Dr Davies retired to Aberystwyth and died there in 1920: the *South Wales Daily Post* edition for 23 August carried an obituary which stated 'Our London correspondent says Dr Morgan Davies was for forty years the medical adviser to a large number of Welsh families in the metropolis.'

In his last few years in Wales, Dr Davies remained what the *Daily Post* called someone who 'did much to foster the young patriots who afterwards became the leaders of Welsh political life'. This showed in the letters he wrote to John Williams, which are stored in the National Library of Wales though not in John Williams's personal archive. One letter, written on 22 May 1894, makes it clear that the two men did indeed know each other. He urges Dr John Williams to help him in his campaign to separate the Welsh medical men from the English practitioners in the listings of *The Medical Directory*, just as the Irish and Scots are. He asks this of John Williams because, he says, he knows of 'your hearty interest in everything related to Wales' – which he would only be aware of if he knew John Williams.

The name of Dr Davies, in relation to Whitechapel and the Ripper murders, is well known already to Ripperologists, although the link comes not from him but from one of the perennial Ripper suspects, Robert D'Onston Stephenson. Stephenson was almost certainly mentally ill and definitely deluded; he was also in the London Hospital from 25 July to 7 December 1888, suffering from 'neurasthenia'. He raised his suspicions about the Ripper with a friend, and then later with Scotland Yard. He told the police that Dr Morgan Davies had been in the ward of the London Hospital where he was staying, and had demonstrated to a 'shocked' Stephenson how the victims had been strangled from behind while being sodomised. (This we know is untrue; none of the victims was assaulted in this way.) There is no indication of the police taking this seriously, and no indication that they visited Dr Davies and asked him for his version of events.

What this does tell us, though, is one very interesting thing. It is generally accepted that Stephenson knew who Dr Davies was, and that Dr Davies was in the ward, demonstrating the murderer's technique; yet we know (from *The Medical Directory*) that he had long ago left their employ. So if he was in the hospital, he would have been merely a visitor to the wards, able to walk in and converse with his fellow doctors, observe the patients, perhaps help with diagnoses and maybe offer some other small kinds of assistance, without being paid or appearing on any official record.

Just as we believe John Williams did in the Workhouse Infirmary.

Dr Davies must have been the Morgan to whom John Williams wrote about his 'clinic', rather than to his brother Morgan, since John Williams felt no need to explain about a 'clinic' miles from where he was officially employed; Dr Davies, who worked alongside him when the great man came to visit the infirmary three years before, would know exactly what Dr Williams meant. Even if he did not know exactly what it was that Dr Williams was intending to do at his 'clinic', or, indeed, how loose a term that had become for John Williams.

The Welsh connections in John Williams's London life extended far beyond Dr Davies, though, thanks to his money. The doctor was amassing an income that allowed him to be an industrious book collector, and he had begun to build his own network of agents and suppliers. We saw that some of this income came from investments in property in the East End; he owned a row of houses in Pendelstone Street, in Walthamstow. As well as relying on stalwarts in London such as Bernard Quaritch, whose business still flourishes, he also had a network of local dealers and collectors who would let him know if they were offered any interesting items of Welsh literary history. Some of the letters from these people, including Quaritch, are in the archive at the National Library. It is obvious that many of his correspondents knew the doctor, and knew his literary tastes and requirements well. So it is safe to assume that he returned regularly to those places where he might expect to meet his dealers and fellow collectors, and to see what else they had to offer.

Many of them would have lived in the South Wales city of Cardiff.

Of course, he could always have visited Cardiff simply to see Dr Andrew Davies, who had been one of the partners in the surgery where John Williams had begun his career. After all, we know from a record of a dinner held in his honour in Wales in 1901 that he was still in touch with the other partner, Dr Ebenezer Davies, so it would not be surprising if he took the time and trouble to see his old friend while in Cardiff. Especially so, given that Dr Andrew Davies was also the Secretary of the South Wales and Monmouthshire Medical Association, and we know that John Williams, as a fervent Welshman, would have supported such an organisation.

On leaving the practice in Swansea, Dr Andrew Davies had taken up residence in Cardiff, next door to the infirmary, which later became Cardiff Hospital. As we know from the census records, he lived with his wife and family. As the former President of the South Wales branch of the BMA it is safe to assume that Dr Davies was a regular visitor to the infirmary next door. Perhaps he took John Williams on his round with him one day? Perhaps, as they wandered round, the visitor from London saw a young woman who caught his eye, a woman who was attractive enough for hard-bitten policemen to mention her good looks wistfully after her death? For it was to an infirmary in Cardiff that Mary Kelly went, after her husband Jonathan had been killed in a mining accident. We do not know why Mary Kelly needed to go to the infirmary – Joe Barnett was not asked and he does not volunteer this information. But if she was in the infirmary she would undoubtedly have been placed in one of the women's wards and it would be there that Dr Andrew Davies would take the doctor who specialised in obstetric medicine, and listen to him offer his expert advice and opinion on interesting cases.

Of course, there is another possibility; Mary Kelly told Joe Barnett that she went into an infirmary in Cardiff, but that once she was out of the infirmary, she had fallen in with her cousin, and it was this woman who introduced her into prostitution. Dr Williams may have met Mary Kelly while she was going about her business, rather than the other way round. If that was the case, then there is nothing surprising about there being no record of their association. Who records their assignations with a prostitute? Either option is as likely, or unlikely, as the other. If Mary Kelly the prostitute met John Williams the eminent doctor, he would have impressed upon her the necessity of remaining silent about his identity. No one would have been surprised by a rich and powerful man looking for a prostitute, even if publicly they condemned it, but it would not have done his career any good if such a thing were widely known. So she would have never broken his confidence, and would not have told Joe Barnett the identity of her 'gentleman', for this would have lost her business. And, at the time, she needed him; as a young widow with a small child, she must have felt that this ageing Welsh doctor was a better prospect for her – at least he could take her away from the confines of Wales and show her the big city. To her, the wealthy married man would have seemed a godsend.

At some point, then, Mary Kelly travelled up to London, perhaps in the company of John Williams. She was said by a newspaper of the time to be living in Knightsbridge; according to some, she was in a house in Cleveland Street. A man named Edmund Bellord claimed to have found Mary Kelly a job in the street there, working in a shop. Cleveland Street lay midway between Queen Anne Street, where John Williams and his wife lived, and UCH, where he worked. The street would not have been more than a five-minute walk from either his home or the hospital where he worked – placing her very close to him indeed.

Perhaps he was determined to keep her near him; maybe that is why she moved into a house in a street halfway between his home and the hospital where he worked. The points of connection between the two of them are such that it seems unlikely to be just a coincidence – firstly, the link in Cardiff, and then living less than five minutes from him in London.

For a while, maybe she was everything Dr John Williams wanted – young, compliant, pretty and lively. There is even a rumour that she spoke Welsh as he did. At some stage, then, he went one step further than simply visiting her in the house where he had installed her; he took her to Paris. A few short years later, when she was in Whitechapel, she told Joe Barnett that she did not like it there and came back to London, but perhaps the truth is that John Williams did not like it there with her; that he realised what a fool he was being with his young mistress, while his wife was alone at home in England. So they returned to London, only for him to abandon her. Without her protector, she was forced to leave the comfortable house she had been living in, in the heart of wealthy and privileged London, and start on her downward path to the East End.

How would John Williams have managed this trip to Paris? John Williams's passport was dated from July 1890 – some years after we suspected that he had taken Mary Kelly to Paris. Consulting books about the use of passports in the later nineteenth century, however, it became clear that he would not have needed one; the passport was only occasionally used (France was the main country in Europe that had insisted on passports, but, apart from the war of 1870-1, did not seem to require them in the decades that interested us). Even the one issued to John Williams – which remained unsigned by him – bore no identification, simply stating that 'Dr John Williams (British Subject) travelling on the Continent' should be allowed free passage. In the past, passports had referred to the holder as an 'English Gentleman travelling with his wife and servants' – so it was clear that even if, as all the evidence suggested, John Williams did not hold a passport until years after he had first travelled on the continent for his honeymoon, neither he nor his companion, Mary, would have been stopped and questioned.

Meanwhile, John Williams perhaps decided to make something of his life with his wife, and maybe they renewed their attempts to have children. Perhaps the previous efforts to do so were now overshadowed by his experience of the rather more worldly Mary Kelly; maybe his disappointment in his wife became more pronounced. It seems commonplace to deride Victorian marriages as fine on the surface, and a hotbed of secrets and recriminations underneath, but it would appear that this was the case with Dr and Mrs Williams. All the evidence points towards an unhappy union for both of them, and, from what we know of his personality, there is no doubt that Lizzie was made to feel his disappointment more acutely than John Williams felt hers.

But maybe there was something else which has not made it into any official records. John Williams's researches, as we discussed in relation to the interests shown by the papers he delivered at the society he had joined, now focused intently upon the function and diseases of the uterus. If he believed that his wife's apparent infertility came from her having suffered from one of these diseases in the past, maybe his increasing scientific interest was coupled with a private desire to seek a cure for her. The doctor would have paid more regular visits to the infirmary in Whitechapel; the sick lay in such numbers here that he was always able to find exactly the kind of patient that matched his wife for age and general condition. Although the murdered women were, with the exception of Mary Kelly, older than Lizzie Williams, newspaper reports from the time state that they appeared younger than their actual age – perhaps making it clear why the doctor selected those particular women, and not some of their equally miserable fellows.

One such patient may have been Catherine Eddowes, who was in the infirmary in 1887. We cannot be certain, as there were no official notes left behind of any work he did in the infirmary – perhaps he kept those papers during the years he worked there but destroyed them after he had left Whitechapel – but we do know that she was there at the time we suspect he was, and he might well have examined her. The only one of the victims whose name he recorded was Mary Ann Nichols, and perhaps he had forgotten that her name was not only in the notes he made at the infirmary but also in the books he liked to use to record details of the patients he saw.

John Williams continued working with the women in the Whitechapel Infirmary right through the 1880s. He had to devote time at the weekends to go there to work with the poor women of those slums, because of the commitments he had elsewhere to UCH, to the other institutions with which he was associated, and to his private patients. But he always valued hard work, and spoke at length about its benefits as well as its certainty in a doctor's lot. Nowhere can have been busier than in the frenetic working environment of the Whitechapel Workhouse Infirmary, where his assistance – particularly his expertise in matters that would have come frequently before the overworked doctor and his junior there – must have been very welcome. Especially as he seemed prepared to contribute so freely of his time, even if he had in the past required them to reimburse him for specialist equipment. It cannot have had rewards for him outside the narrow confines of his research, for, as Charles Booth wrote about the poor of the district, 'Their life is the life of savages, with vicissitudes of extreme hardship and occasional excess. Their food is of the coarsest description, and their only luxury is drink. It is not easy to say how they live.'

The discoveries at the Royal Society of Obstetricians and Gynaecologists, and the subsequent information gathered from the Whitechapel Infirmary led us to consider something else. Here was an institution devoted to the poor, in the district where the women who were killed were among the very poorest. Was it possible that there would be some link between these women and the infirmary? The only official connection we had come across so far was that the body of Mary Ann Nichols, the first victim, ended up in the Whitechapel Infirmary when it was taken to the mortuary after she was found on the street.

Perhaps by then John Williams had left for the West End, and home; perhaps he busied himself elsewhere in the infirmary? We do know that the initial assumptions of the police would have excluded him automatically. Abberline, the Detective in charge of the case, wrote about the murder of the second victim, Annie Chapman, and the claim that the killer was a man who knew her, one Edward Stanley. He said that it would not be right to be suspicious of him as 'he was a respectable hard-working man'. With such ready assumptions, who would challenge a high-ranking doctor such as John Williams?

We looked again at the reports of the victims' lives, and decided to work methodically through all we knew of them. To start with, our investigations were easy. Mary Ann Nichols, it was widely noted, had spent most of the last few years of her life living in workhouses, mostly in Lambeth, for she featured often enough in the records of the institution there. It was because the name of the workhouse was stitched into her undergarments that she was identified in the first place. Besides that, she was named by John Williams himself in one of his notebooks. So far, so good. However, Annie Chapman did not appear to have been to the infirmary, though she did use a variety of names, as did many of the women. Annie was involved in a fight about three days before she died and declared then that she was going to go to the infirmary to seek treatment.

The infirmary records deposited at the London Metropolitan Archive include the Admissions and Discharge books for 1888. As you might imagine, these have been heavily studied over the years, and it is now no longer possible to see the volume for the second half of 1888. It is being restored, and, because of the backlog of materials, this may well take years. Although we were not able to see for ourselves if Annie Chapman's name (or any of her pseudonyms) showed up in that book, to date no other accounts of the Ripper's crimes mention finding her name in that or any other workhouse records.

There is another possibility. Not only do we know that people turned up at the infirmary and refused to give their names, as happened in 1884, for example, when questions were asked in the House of Commons about the role of the workhouse; but we also know there was a back entrance. It is through this entrance that John Williams might have left the premises, unobtrusively, to walk the streets. Again, the records are clear that there is a back entrance because during 1888 twenty-year-old Edward Maloney escaped through it. Security within the workhouse premises was never particularly good – as the sad example of Betsy Wilks who burned herself to death showed. So is it possible that Annie Chapman was able to gain entrance to the infirmary without having her name recorded? She had pills on her when she died; she spilled them and collected them up in a scrap of paper which led to two innocent soldiers being questioned about her death. She must have got these pills from somewhere; given that she declared she was going to the infirmary, it is impossible to believe they came from anywhere else.

In the lists of people up in front of the magistrates for various offences at the workhouse, the name 'John Kelly' appeared a number of times. Kelly was the lover of Catherine Eddowes, the third victim. Catherine herself appears in the records of the infirmary under one of her surnames, which she had taken from her first lover and the father of her children, Thomas Conway. She was inside the infirmary, for a 'burn of foot', on 14-20 June 1887. Her address was given as a house in Flower and Dean Street.

But there was another, more intriguing connection with Catherine Eddowes that we came across early on in our researches, and which we tried hard to track down. When we read the *Transactions of the Obstetrical Society of Great Britain,* we noted the firm relationship we could establish through its pages between John Williams, and his two friends Dr Champneys and Dr Herman.

Dr Champneys, because of his father – and we felt there was likely to be a family connection with Dr A.M. Champneys –

could already be linked to Whitechapel. Dr Herman, like Dr Francis Champneys, was a friend of John Williams, although the two men appear never to have worked at the same institution together – at least on paper. However, they collaborated on papers for the Obstetrical Society and we can see that Champneys and Herman were strong supporters of John Williams when he was pressing his case or, indeed, when he was made President of the Society. Under his presidency, the two men became joint Secretaries to the Society. The fact that the three men worked together on their papers was noted by the *Lancet* in the 23 June issue, 1888. But the key thing about Dr Herman is that he worked at the London Hospital – and that he took patients, and, in late 1887, one patient in particular, from the hospital where Dr Champneys and John Williams both worked, the Lying-In Hospital in Waterloo. And what was particularly fascinating about this patient? She was suffering from a disease of the kidneys known as Bright's disease, an inflammation of the kidneys now known as nephritis.

Catherine Eddowes was suffering from Bright's disease, and Eddowes was the victim whose mutilation included not only the removal of part of her uterus but also her kidneys. It was supposedly her kidney that was posted to George Lusk, the chair of the vigilante committee in Whitechapel.

When we read this, we wondered what we had found. John Williams had made a special study of Bright's disease when he was training to become a doctor – it was possible to see this when looking through some of his medical notebooks in the National Library in Aberystwyth. But when we started to look for evidence that this woman – unnamed by Dr Herman – was Catherine Eddowes, we found nothing, and she remained anonymous. However, just as we were about to give up our search, and admit to failing to find a connection between her and the infirmary, she turned up, in the Admissions and Discharge book from the workhouse infirmary. As with Annie Chapman, we looked for her under some of her other names;

and there was Catherine Conway, in the infirmary in 1887. Catherine Eddowes had, tattooed on her arm, the initials of the father of her children: TC, or Thomas Conway.

So now we had traced the link between Mary Kelly and John Williams. We also knew that Polly Nichols had seen John Williams; and that Annie Chapman, and Catherine Eddowes had been patients in the infirmary at one time or another. This left us with Liz Stride; and every account we read of her life states that she was living in the infirmary during 1881 when she was suffering from bronchitis. This was obviously much earlier than any of the connections with the infirmary that we had so far been looking into, but we do know that John Williams had been associating with Dr Ilott from the infirmary since 1877.

In Whitechapel, we stood where the old infirmary buildings had once housed all those sick and dying people. We walked to all the murder sites, timing the trips. Even on a busy afternoon with everyone scurrying along to get out of the cold air, it did not take long to walk briskly from the infirmary to each of the murder sites. Durward Street – where Mary Ann Nichols was found – was less than two minutes away, with the places where Annie Chapman and Mary Kelly died not more than a five- or ten-minute walk. The murder site furthest away from the infirmary was that of Catherine Eddowes, at nearly fifteen minutes, but of course this was also a convenient distance from the place where, on the same night she was killed, Liz Stride died; convenient, that is, in taking the killer away from the hue and cry that arose once Liz Stride's body was discovered. We knew that in the early hours of the morning the streets would be a lot less busy, allowing the murderer to move quickly down the dark alleyways, and return to the sanctuary of the infirmary.

It was possible now to place John Williams at the infirmary, with a written connection to Mary Ann Nichols; then Annie Chapman with her pills; and Catherine Eddowes and Liz Stride, who both had recorded entries in the infirmary's records. Surely this meant that our deductions were correct; the first four victims were in Whitechapel in the infirmary, and the doctor was there alongside them.

There was one vexing question about the victims and one that remains crucial: *for what reason* had they been killed? We did not feel that the Ripper was a sadistic murderer, as so many other solutions suggested – the women were all killed *before* their bodies were mutilated – but there was something about the women themselves that prompted the man to kill them. John Williams wanted something specific from them; these women were not picked out at random to die. At the time, some people thought this was a possibility too; one writer to *The Times* of 26 September 1888 said he thought that the killer could not be 'a drunken loafer' but was more likely 'a person making research from motives of science or curiosity'.

John Williams himself wrote that, 'The best scientific work does not meet with an immediate visible and palpable reward.' The doctor would have looked at these women as nothing more than cases to be examined, symptoms to be understood, greater knowledge to be sought. He encountered them in the course of his work at the infirmary, and something about them – or maybe about their diseases – drew him to them. Knowing what he spoke about at the Obstetrical Society meetings, what he wrote his papers about, what he was researching, will give us an inkling of what exactly interested him about them so much.

We went through the papers that we had collected which dealt with John Williams's published work. His research papers show that he had chosen to focus on the uterus, its functions, and the diseases it was prone to. We already knew that he was remembered in the medical world chiefly for his use of abdominal operations, so we can assume that he chose to investigate the uterus and its complications with both surgical and internal examinations. But why did he need to go further with the women who died at his hands, and what did he expect to learn from them that he could not have learned within the walls of the infirmary?

He wanted something specific from these women, and we believe that what John Williams wanted more than anything else was to understand the function of the ovaries, their relation to fertility, and to see if he could perhaps use the organs he removed from the women to complete his research. Maybe he even wanted to go so far as to transplant these fertile organs into his sterile wife. We have no evidence of this, but it is a distinct possibility, given the remarks of Dr Matthews Duncan, the President of the Obstetrical Society, who said that he used to think curing sterility was impossible but had lately come to the view that it was 'sometimes cured'.

Chapter Fourteen

As the end of the decade approached, John Williams was employed at University College Hospital, where he not only saw patients but taught students; as with many of the doctors based here, he also worked at the St Pancras and Northern Dispensary near the hospital. In addition to this, he ran the Lying-In Hospital in Waterloo, along with his friend Dr Francis Champneys; was a busy member of committees at the Society of Obstetricians, and, for a two-year period covering 1888, its President; an honorary member of other societies, with whom he would have been in correspondence; and on top of all that, he ran a private practice, which had to take priority over these other activities as this was the real source of his income.

However, his private practice blossomed when he was given the ultimate accolade, and appointed to the royal family to serve as the physician *accoucheur* to Princess Beatrice, the Queen's youngest daughter. Apart from this being a terrific feather in his cap in terms of London society, it would have meant that he could charge more for his time, and that he could rid himself of some of his more disagreeable activities. Or so one would have thought.

In addition to all this work noted in *The Medical Directory*, John Williams made regular visits to Whitechapel to work at the infirmary there. We have, in the form of a letter he wrote to one of his contacts there, the doctor's own word to confirm that this is the case.

What was his state of mind as he approached his mid forties, and what pressures must he have put himself under in his search for recognition and – who knows? – something more? There were mutterings within the medical community about his appointment to the position of physician *accoucheur* to the Princess. He was not popular, and some doctors, just like many other professionals, were envious of those who achieved things they would wish for themselves. Yet it *is* extraordinary that he should have been appointed. Why was he preferred? He was not at the top of his profession. There were many other obstetricians who were more highly thought of than John Williams; he was not from a well-to-do family who would already be connected with the society in which the Queen and her daughters moved. Does it say much for the egalitarian spirit of the age that the doctor from a farm in the Welsh valleys was chosen, just as the leader of the Conservative Party at the beginning of that decade was Jewish and just as much an outsider as John Williams? Perhaps he was chosen simply because he would be thought sufficiently grateful to be so recognised that he would always keep the confidence of the Queen and her family. Perhaps the other doctors were thought unsuitable for one reason or another, and John Williams was the least bad alternative.

Whatever the answer, he would have found himself reaching the pinnacle of his career, while at the same time facing ever-increasing hostility from certain sections of the medical profession: an interesting combination of circumstances that must have seemed very trying to John Williams. He could not turn to Lizzie, his wife, for support at this difficult time; while outwardly there was no show of it, and therefore no record in letters or journals that we can consult, their marriage was doubtless deteriorating. She was probably aware he had had relationships with women outside the marriage, and that her continued inability to bear children provoked him. We believe this partly because she receives so little notice from him in the documents that survive, partly from the information that has been passed down the family, and partly from what we can detect from photographs of them at that stage in their marriage. The albums are filled, moreover, with large numbers of photographs of children, given to him by his grateful patients.

During 1887-8 the pressure on him increased enormously. Within the Obstetrical Society, although he was bolstered by the support of his friends Dr Herman and Dr Champneys, he was not a popular President, and the antagonistic Dr Graily Hewitt, among others, continued to snipe at what he saw as wrong-headedness in Dr Williams's work. He carried on with his exhausting workload, reluctant to relinquish any role that might enhance his reputation in front of his private patients and maintain his earning power. Of course, it could also be said that he did not give up any of his roles because any one of them might have led him to a medical discovery, making him very successful and even popular. He would also not have given up any work that might have helped him uncover the mystery of his wife's sterility.

It is not surprising then that his commitment to the infirmary in Whitechapel remained strictly a voluntary one, in that he could not afford the time to be made an official member of staff, even if it had been legally possible to do so (it was not); his relationship with the institution remained in his hands only. It would have been to the advantage of the two doctors working in the infirmary to have his experience, let alone having another pair of hands to deal with the seven hundred or so patients held within its walls every day, and so it is likely that they would have been willing to work with him on his terms. Dr Herbert Larder had replaced Dr Ilott, and for most of the time preceding the murders Dr Larder had as his assistant Dr Walter Arthur, who started in May 1887; but Dr Arthur resigned on grounds of ill health on 18 September 1888. He was replaced in early October by Dr John E. Gould, who was already familiar with the infirmary as he had worked there over the summer months, providing cover for Dr Larder and Dr Arthur while they were away on their summer holidays.

Therefore, the doctors who now worked in the infirmary would have been introduced to Dr John Williams as someone who had been coming to the infirmary over many years, his freedom to visit the place a long-established tradition that a newcomer would feel he had no right to revoke. Nor would they be surprised to see his face within its walls at odd hours of the day or night; they would have known about his busy working life elsewhere, and he would have been allowed to come and go as he pleased, just as he had always done.

So what sort of person was John Williams? It is difficult to establish what kind of character he was. He was a good host for his fellow doctors, entertaining them at his club; he was firm and unyielding in his opinions, and this sometimes rubbed up people the wrong way. Not enough is known about what went on inside his head, and as he had taken pains to remove pages from the 1888 diary (which, until the pages were removed, was filled more substantially than all his diaries), nothing can be gleaned from these sources. Remarks he made in passing indicated that he barely tolerated people he considered beneath him, in terms of their intelligence and capacity for hard work, but no more could be deduced than this.

Equally difficult to ascertain is the true nature of his relationship with Mary Kelly. The fact that the relationship had rocked his marriage enough for it to be recalled a hundred years later meant that it had obviously been an important one. We know that it was enough to take the girl away from everything she knew – including, quite possibly, her child – and so it was more than just a passing fancy for both of them.

If John Williams was a doctor who killed, even if he felt these deaths were necessary in the cause of his research, was he any different from doctors who kill because it gives them some kind of thrill? Was it possible that he had killed before 1888 – that his victims died on the operating table, rather than on the street, and that instead of being castigated as a criminal he was hailed as a pioneer? Would the women who died under his knife – and there would undoubtedly have been some who did – have felt themselves to be victims any the less if they knew that their deaths were going to enable other women to live? And if he, Dr Williams, allowed himself to think like that, would he have worried about a few sad old prostitutes who were almost certainly going to die in a miserable way in the next few years anyway?

Previous writers on the subject have always agreed that there was no connection between any of the victims, and that their murderer was not known to any of them – that they were strangers, killed by a stranger. Only one popular theory has ever tried to suggest otherwise, and it was offered by Stephen Knight, who alleged that the women conspired together to blackmail the Crown over the illegitimate royal baby sired on Catholic Annie Crook. No one takes this theory seriously any more.

But what if all the victims were linked not just in death but also in life by their killer? Suppose that first Liz Stride, then Mary Ann Nichols, then Catherine Eddowes, then Annie Chapman, all came before John Williams in his role as doctor during his time at the infirmary? We know that Mary Ann Nichols did; we know that the other three women were all in the infirmary at some point. And suppose that the final victim had inadvertently been selected long before, several years ago, when she had made the mistake of taking up with a rich doctor. We are not suggesting that John Williams had planned the murder of these women over many years; merely that the women (who – apart from Mary Kelly – were all looked about the same age as his wife) made the mistake of being the wrong patients, in the wrong place, at the wrong time.

No one who met him in the streets outside the workhouse infirmary in the autumn of 1888 was ready to question Dr John Williams about his presence in Whitechapel. The doctor was a regular fixture at the infirmary; provided he had no other reason to be at home or out of town he would turn up at the infirmary. Sometimes he would spend long hours there into the night, carrying out the research he could not do earlier in the week on account of his other commitments. Perhaps he kept working then because it kept him away from the home that increasingly depressed him. His determination to do something about his wife's condition, as well as to make his name, must have increased as the years went by; his failure to do anything for her or for himself must have become increasingly difficult to bear.

So, a demoralised, overworked Dr Williams willingly takes himself away from his home to visit his occasional clinic in Whitechapel one August evening. Whitechapel is bustling day and night; being close to the docks there is a constant need to provide food, drink and other necessities to the thousands of visiting sailors and dockyard workers. Dr Williams arrives in Whitechapel to find it as busy as ever; he becomes anonymous in the crowd, a familiar sight over the last eight or so years. He is not accosted by the streetwalkers; they know he is not looking for their custom. They recognise him as someone who has been as intimate as any paying customer, but, unlike those men, his interest in them is not for sexual gratification. By comparison, his interests seem almost altruistic. Perhaps one or two of them stop him to tell him about their illnesses; perhaps they know only too well that it is this aspect of their bodies that truly animates him. Maybe he even recognises one of them, Polly Nichols, who came to him a few years ago with a baby, and left without one? Does she smile at him? Does she exhibit the same signs of an early pregnancy, one that only a doctor could see? Does he feel angry to think he left his fine but barren wife in their fine but empty home, only to come here to see some fecund whore flaunt her pregnancy at him?

He walks through the infirmary this August evening; the staff there change with alarming frequency, and after the many years he spent alongside Dr Ilott he has found it easier to go straight to the separate building, housing the mortuary and the post-mortem room, where he keeps his research jars and instruments, rather than spend time with Dr Larder, the officious new doctor in charge of the infirmary. He settles himself, and begins to calm down. So what if Polly Nichols is pregnant? What does that matter to him? Unless ... what if he could learn something from this? What if Polly, who is probably dying of some disease or other anyway, could be parted from her womb, so that his wife, a much more deserving case, could benefit? After all, women had died before by his hand; women who were nearly dead anyway, but whose life expectancy, instead of being lengthened by surgery, had been radically shortened. No one had missed them; who would miss Polly Nichols?

We do not know what John Williams did now; had he seen Polly earlier in the evening and arranged for the two of them to meet later? Did he know long before then that he was going to have to kill someone, to keep his research alive?

When he had done so, what use would the parts of their bodies he removed be to him? How did he manage to evade notice and capture when all of Whitechapel was out hunting for Jack the Ripper? And, most importantly of all, what convinced him to stop committing these crimes?

The police were in every nook and cranny of Whitechapel by the time of Mary Kelly's death; Queen Victoria herself had written to the Home Secretary to express her worries about the ongoing situation in the East End. The police had visited the infirmary; Inspector Abberline wrote in September about visits to 'the London Hospital and other places', but had to admit that 'no useful information has been obtained'. Vigilante groups roamed the streets and alleyways at night; the area was unsafe for almost any single man to walk through, as he would be set upon by the mob and only if he was lucky be turned over to the police. John Williams knew it was no longer a safe place for him to visit; he had, in any event, succumbed to the madness of his dissection of Mary Kelly, which marked some sort of resolution in his own unhappy mind and which, perhaps, in the ferocity of his assault, laid bare the anger and despair he must have felt at not finding a solution to the mystery of sterility that plagued him. The evil that he had done, and the monomania that had foisted it upon him, caused him to have a breakdown that took him away from UCH and his other duties. After taking no part in any of the meetings for the months of October and November with the Society of Obstetricians, John Williams returned to the meeting in early December but made no further presentations of papers, then – or ever again.

So if these are among the reasons John Williams stopped committing the crimes, what was it that caused him to start? We have assumed that he saw a woman he knew and that something about their shared past – the fact that he had helped her when her child had aborted – meant that he knew she had the ability to reproduce, and understanding of this is what he craved. Something drove him to think that a woman of this kind – in her forties, fertile – would have the answers to the problems he was facing. And when this Polly Nichols did not, he was driven on, to find others, others that he knew about, any one of whom could have held the secret that he longed for within the confines of her body. A kind of mania overtook him, and he no longer saw them as alive but as people he knew were sick and dying – albeit slowly – and whose deaths might benefit the lives of many, many more.

Dr John Williams was never Jack the Ripper. Jack the Ripper never existed; his name, as is well known today, was coined by two newspaper reporters (the police believed them to be the authors of some of the supposed Ripper 'letters' as well; many letters were written by hoaxers, including one woman, who was arrested in Bradford), and, although they never accused them, they suspected Tom Bulling of the Central News, and his boss, Charles Moore, of being behind the creation of the dreadful name. The reporters knew only too well that the story of the killer roaming the streets of Whitechapel was too good an opportunity to miss. 'Jack the Ripper' became the name given to the killer by the newspapers because, then as now, a killer with a name like that sold papers. Dr John Williams was never the Ripper of public legend because he did not set out to sadistically kill for some kind of sexual pleasure – all of the women were strangled and their throats cut *before* any mutilations took place

– and because he did not seek to create the kind of panic and terror on the streets of Whitechapel that ensued from the killings. John Williams was a doctor, a surgeon, and as such used to the touch of death in his hands; but he was not a man who was prepared for the furore that the killings brought about. Who would have thought that a handful of prostitutes could have caused such an international outcry, and toppled from his post the head of the Metropolitan Police Force? John Williams did not foresee the outcome of what he had started. This, too, led to his breakdown at the end of 1888, and it was this – as much as anything else – which brought about the end of the murderer's crimes.

The countless women that had passed through his hands since he became a surgeon would have meant little to John Williams, other than those with the potential to improve his lot, either through their wealth and position in society, or those from whom he could gain medical insights. The ambitious man would not have cared about the women in Whitechapel except for what they could give him, and what he could learn from them. For the vast majority of the inhabitants of London, the lives of a few prostitutes were a matter of complete indifference to them. To John Williams, they would not have mattered at all. When the police visited the workhouse to question the staff and the inhabitants about the killings, as we know they did, they would not have been suspicious of the well-to-do doctor, even if he had been present – the staff in the infirmary would not have brought him to the attention of the police because he had been coming to the infirmary for years before the murders started. No one believed that the killer was anything other than a deranged maniac, and probably a foreign one to boot. Only the more thoughtful members of the police doubted this: Inspector Abberline, speaking some fifteen years after the murders were committed, said, 'You must understand that we never believed all those stories about Jack the Ripper being dead, or that he was a lunatic, or anything of that kind. No; the identity of the diabolical individual has yet to be established, notwithstanding the people who have produced these rumours and who pretend to know the state of the official mind.' Whereas another account wrote, 'It was in accordance with current belief in British pride and moral superiority, that no Christian Englishman could have perpetrated such abominations; therefore it *must* have been a foreigner.'

In his memoir, Detective Ben Leeson, a man who joined the police force around the time of the murders, wrote: 'Amongst the police who were most concerned with the case, there was a general feeling that a certain doctor, known to me, could have thrown quite a lot of light on the subject. This particular doctor was never far away when the crimes were committed and it is certain that the injuries inflicted on the victims could only have been done by one skilled in the use of the knife.' Perhaps the police suspected more than has ever been known; but their suspicions could not be made into evidence against their suspect.

So the doctor had settled upon his victims; they were women he saw around the streets of Whitechapel, and women whom he had at some point examined. He knew something about them and what they could offer him, so they were not going to be frightened of him when he approached them – particularly once the whole district was awash with people who had set out to capture the Ripper, or at least to frighten him off. Apart from the vigilante groups that had formed, men came to Whitechapel with the aim of catching the killer or understanding the women he preyed upon. One man dressed up as a woman, hoping to entice the Ripper; instead he was chased by a mob who thought he was the killer. Another, a doctor dressed in 'a jersey in place of a coat, his face most palpably artificially blacked', a disguise that fooled only the mob who chased him into the arms of the police. If Polly Nichols, or Annie Chapman, or Catherine Eddowes, or Liz Stride, was approached by Dr John Williams, they would not be frightened at first – here was someone they knew, someone they trusted. They would not have balked at

moving away from the busy streets and going into dark alleyways and small yards with him, even at a time when they knew
the risks. He was a doctor; he had been there for years; what
could possibly go wrong? Policeman Walter Dew wrote:

> Let us assume for a moment that he [the killer] was a man of
> prominence and good repute locally. Against such a man, in
> the absence of direct evidence, it is too much to expect that
> local police officers would hold such a terrible suspicion.
> And, assuming this to be the case, the man's amazing immu-
> nity can be the more readily explained. The same qualities
> which silenced the suspicions of his women victims would
> keep him right with the police officers who knew and
> respected him.

Walter Dew's words show that the police were not far off
the mark. He also noted that the killings took place on bank
holidays – 'does it mean these two nights were deliberately chosen?' – and that the killer was too 'clever, calculated and
cunning' to be responsible for the illiterate letters claiming to be
from the Ripper that the police received.

The killer was spotted once; at least, it is thought that one of
the witnesses who claimed to have seen the killer was genuine.
George Hutchinson knew Mary Kelly and saw her on the night
of her murder with a man whom he described as about thirty-
four or thirty-five, 5'6" in height, a moustache, long dark coat,
and respectable in appearance. He also mentions a red stone on
the man's coat.

John Williams's friend and colleague, Herbert R. Spencer,
wrote about the doctor and the way he used to dress in London,
in an article which appeared after the Welshman's death. He
describes him as he knew him in London in the late 1880s: he
was of middle height, robust build, he usually wore a frock coat,
silk hat, stand-up collar and a dark silk tie held by a pin set with
a red stone.

Once in private, John Williams immediately killed the women by strangling them and then slitting their throats, which meant that they could not cry out, and that they did not bleed profusely on to him. The fact that most of the wounds were seen to be cuts from left to right suggested to many that the killer was left-handed. The statue of John Williams in the National Library in Aberystwyth shows him holding the plans for the library in his left hand. However, it is more likely that the killer stood behind his victims, perhaps following them into the place they suggested for their assignation, and strangled them and cut their throats from behind. This would have the double benefit of surprise as well as keeping their blood away from him.

The knife used in the murders was, according to the doctor Thomas Bond (who carried out the post-mortem on Mary Kelly), 'of the same character' in all the murders with the exception of Liz Stride's – the assumption of many writers is that the haste with which the Ripper acted in her case means there was not enough evidence for Dr Bond to state it was the same knife. It was 'a strong knife, at least six inches long, very sharp, pointed at the top, and about an inch in width'. It may have been a surgeon's knife, he said, but 'I think it was no doubt a straight knife'.

This is the knife that I had held in my hand back in the reading room of the National Library in Aberystwyth. I am sure of it.

The library's listing of two of the items contained in these boxes is on page 301 of their catalogue of John Williams's archive. It simply states, 'Knife with black handle' and '3 microscopic smears in small wooden box'. Until we can go into the library with the right equipment, and the right experts, we cannot be certain what these items will do to our case.

These two items from that box have gripped our imagination more than any others. The slides, wedged under tiny slivers of glass, contain what is very evidently animal – rather than plant – matter. More than that, we cannot say. Alongside them in the box is a wooden-handled knife, about six or so inches long. It is difficult to be more sure than that because the tip has snapped off. The knife is old, but it is not a kitchen knife, or a garden knife; the blade widens just after leaving the wooden handle to about one inch or so before tapering down to the point. It is still razor sharp.

Why would you keep such a knife? Surely such an eminent and wealthy surgeon would have gone through many, many knives and scalpels in a whole career of performing operations? Why keep this one in a collection of what were mainly documents? What made it so special, considering it was so battered and well used? And why would he keep such a thing when he had given up practising surgery so many years before? Is it possible that, on the knife, there are any traces remaining of what it had once cut?

And those slides. Why, after a professional career spanning decades, were those three slides there, among the final artefacts of this man's life? Would the slides not be more use in the teaching hospital he worked in? What possible use could they have for him? And, if we were able to examine them under a microscope today, what could they show us? Would it be possible to determine whether or not it was human material under that glass, and from what part of the body that material had come from? Was it from a woman? Would it be possible to prove something with it?

These questions are not ones that either of us is able to answer. It is as frustrating now as it has been since we first placed them on the desk in front of us. To hold the knife in our hands as John Williams must have held it is a chilling moment. We are in no doubt as to why he kept this knife. Perhaps for years it had sat harmlessly in his desk drawer for him to cut string, but we believe it had a use well before that time. *In every respect* this knife matches the one described by Dr Thomas Bond.

Using this knife, after the murders, John Williams would have been able to carry out the mutilations to the bodies, obtaining from them what he wanted. Given the nature of some of the mutilations (leaving aside those to Mary Kelly), and the speed at which they were carried out, taking into account the darkness and the prospect of discovery at any moment, it seems unlikely to us that the killer could be anyone other than a doctor. The police did look at this possibility, and medical students throughout the capital were examined with a view to establishing whether or not they could be the killer. One newspaper carried reports of a doctor from Birmingham being arrested at Euston, but no follow-up to his arrest exists. Senior doctors such as John Williams were not considered suspects. They were respected members of society, usually Freemasons and therefore known to their fellow Freemasons in the police and judiciary; they were people of standing in their community who could not possibly commit crimes of this kind. We are less likely to take this point of view today, and yet we are still shocked when doctors such as Harold Shipman are shown to be serial killers. Who would, then, back in the 1880s, have suspected a man such as John Williams?

Mary Kelly was by far the youngest of the other victims, the prettiest, and she died in her own home. Why did John Williams kill her? Was she a greater target than the other women because she had tempted him – or was it because she was some kind of threat to him? Could she have identified him? In her last few days, according to Joe Barnett, she was very frightened of the Ripper and asked Joe to read to her from the newspaper about him. Did she suspect her former lover? Had she seen him, at night, walking along with one of the women who later died? And why, when she died, did he defile her body in the way he did? The sight of her corpse is horrific – but does it look any different from any other body dissected by a student in a hospital? Was this last act of the murderer an attempt to mark some kind of completion of his 'work'? Is this mutilation a link with the

Bible, and so also to Freemasons, claimed by many who are fascinated by the Ripper's crimes?

The Freemasons have been seen as a sinister organisation over the years in part because the institutions around them have felt threatened by the idea of an organisation that owes them no allegiance. In John Williams's time, this view was particularly prevalent in the Catholic Church, which wanted to resist any force that might have the practical effect of limiting its power. Pope Leo XIII had, in 1884, issued the '*Humanum Genus*' which attacked all those opposed to the Church as allies of Satan, but in particular the Freemasons: 'In our days, however, those who follow the evil one seem to conspire and strive all together under the guidance and with the help of that society of men spread all over, and solidly established, which they call Free Masons.'

Merely raising the Freemasons in connection with the Ripper murders risks an element of ridicule. The association between the two stems from the widely discredited theory that the Freemasons organised a defence of the Crown (against a possible Catholic threat to the succession) by murdering the five prostitutes who knew about the illegitimate Catholic baby supposedly sired by a royal prince. There will always be people who would like to believe this conspiracy theory, in spite of all evidence to the contrary, and we were confident throughout our research that we would be able to ignore any masonic involvement as merely a flight of fancy.

Until, that is, we compared a passage from the doctor's report given at the inquest into her death with a passage from the Bible. We wondered whether there was any link between the apparently mindless destruction of Mary Kelly's body and the religious element of John Williams's life.

Whether it was some kind of signal to fellow masons it is difficult to know. If the killer was acting with these thoughts in his mind, then he would have to know the appropriate passages from Leviticus and what they meant very well in order to recall them while engaged in such vile slaughter. Bearing in mind that John Williams was the son of a preacher, and had been brought up by his mother to enter the priesthood himself, he most certainly would have known his Bible.

We compared the two passages:

And he shall bring his trespass offering unto the Lord for his sin which he hath sinned, a female from the flock …
for a sin offering …

And he shall bring them unto the priest, who shall offer that which is for the sin offering first, and wring off his head from his neck, but not divide it asunder …

And he shall offer the second for a burnt offering, according to the manner: and the priest shall make an atonement for him for his sin which he hath sinned, and it shall be forgiven him. (Leviticus 5: 6, 8, 10)

The 'manner' is specified in Leviticus 7: 2–4:

In the place where they kill the burnt offering shall they kill the trespass offering: and the blood thereof shall he sprinkle round about upon the altar.

And he shall offer of it all the fat thereof; the rump, and the fat that covereth the inwards.

And the two kidneys, and the fat that is on them, which is by the flanks, and the caul that is above the liver, with the kidneys, it shall he take away.

Mary Kelly was a prostitute, and we believe a mistress to John Williams; was she a 'trespass offering'? At her inquest, the following details were revealed:

The body was lying naked in the middle of the bed … The whole of the surface of the abdomen and thighs was removed and the abdominal cavity emptied of its viscera.

The breasts were cut off, the arms mutilated by several jagged wounds and the face hacked beyond recognition of the features. The tissues of the neck were severed all round down to the bone.

The skin and tissues of the abdomen from the costal arch to the pubes were removed in three large flaps. The right thigh was denuded in front to the bone, the flap of skin including the external organs of generation, and part of the right buttock. The left thigh was stripped of skin fascia, and muscles as far as the knee.

The pericardium was open below and the heart absent.

As we know, in the room where she died, there were traces of a large fire in the grate, so hot that it had melted off the spout of a kettle. Her heart was missing; and was never found. Though the ashes of the fire were carefully sifted, according to the press reports, no sign of human remains was discovered. We cannot rely on the rumours that abounded in the press at the time, but no other theory sufficient to explain the excessive heat of the fire has been put forward.

We looked for accounts of nineteenth-century dissections in the libraries that we visited. Unsurprisingly, perhaps, the available books are rather coy on the subject. One of the modern-day books for medical students remarks that this is a difficult area for most new students to accept. It suggests that the student starts the dissection with the cadaver face down on the table so that the student can gain experience of dissection without the traumatic moment of cutting into the face of a person. Also, more practically, they add that the skin on the back is thinner, and can therefore be more easily removed for the student to begin working on the layers below.

One thing is irrefutable: her mutilation went far beyond that of the other women. Of course, it could be argued that this fate only befell her because the other women were killed on the street, and her killer had the space and time to carry out his work in private. But the reports of her death and the two photographs that exist suggest something deeper, something more personal, in the frenzied attack on her dead body. If, as we suspect, she knew John Williams, did she also suspect he was the Ripper – and was she planning to blackmail him? Was she going to expose him, as an adulterer – or even a murderer? Or was this a crime that had less to do with her and more with him; the killer wanted to make this the final murder, and the resemblance between her mutilations and the lines from the Bible was no coincidence but a ritual carried out to mark the conclusion – and to send out a signal to those who would recognise it, that the 'atonement' had taken place?

The doctor who praised 'hard work' and 'stamina' in his speech to the young students in Wales would have been capable of working through the night, and so as a regular visitor would have returned to the infirmary with impunity. He would have had his own entrance and even, perhaps, his own key to the post-mortem room, where he would have carefully stored the organs that he had removed from his victims. Perhaps he even placed them in a jar which he then carried out, past the policeman standing outside the front entrance, before hailing a cab to return home to his wife. She would not have suspected him, and, even if she had, she would certainly not have reported him to the police. John Williams was a man used to being obeyed; 'he asserts himself aggressively,' we are told by the anonymous biographer from *Gentlewoman* magazine in 1891. So he would return, take his specimen down to his own surgery, and examine it there for what he hoped it would reveal to him.

At some point, perhaps when he felt the police came too close to him, the sheer awfulness, the magnitude, of what he was doing must have overwhelmed him. He had been oppressed by the mutterings within the profession against him, as well as by the absence of children in his marriage. Once he had embarked on his murders in the East End, he could not stop until he had marked their end in some way – as the corpse of Mary Kelly and the way it had been mutilated indicated – and it was only then that he could confront the terrible realisation of what he had done. The first thing he did, once he had recovered from his nervous collapse, and to which he alluded in his letter to Sophia Owen, was to put temptation behind him. He asked to be moved to work in the out-patients department at UCH on Saturday mornings, so preventing himself from having the freedom to travel east to Whitechapel at those times. Soon after that he asked the board at UCH to be excused from performing ovariotomies, and wrote to his patients across London to say the same thing. He made almost no further contributions to the Obstetrical Society's meetings, and, when he had completed his term of office as President, made no attempt to present papers or to quiz his fellows after their presentations. It is as if, almost overnight, he lost interest altogether in what had been driving his ambition for the last twenty years.

Back in Whitechapel, Dr Loane, the Medical Officer for Health for Whitechapel, made his annual report to the Local Government Board in Whitehall. He noted that the number of deaths in the district of Whitechapel was low – 1574 from a population that stood at around 74,500. The largest number of deaths came from the newborns; after that, it was those in the forty-sixty age bracket, around 19.7 per cent. The year 1888 had been particularly bad for violence in the area:

You will perceive that we suffer somewhat more from constitutional and respiratory diseases, and also from violence, but the latter, as you are aware, is a very unusual distinction. During the year the civilized world heard with horror of the terrible outrages that took place in Whitechapel. All bore the same evidence that one person was concerned, and that person was without doubt a lunatic. It is also clear to those who are familiar with the District, that were the miscreant a resident in the district, he could not have escaped detection.

John Williams temporarily settled back into his life of practising at UCH and, for a short while only, at a small number of other institutions. In 1893 he resigned from UCH and gave up all other kinds of work in public hospitals. For the next few years, he devoted himself entirely to the private patients that were going to help fund his retirement, and he continued to assist the Queen in attending the births of more royal children. The reversal of his enterprising and ambitious career is sudden. At the end of 1888, he is at the height of his powers; within four years, he had abandoned almost all his public work. He claimed 'poor health' forced him to retire from UCH, but he continued to practise privately and to work for the royal family for many years afterwards, and he was a tireless and vigorous campaigner for the National Library of Wales well into the next century. Add to this the fact that he lived for another thirty-three years after his 'retirement', and the state of his health does seem a somewhat incredible excuse for retiring.

Why this sudden decline in his work? Did he recoil from performing ovariotomies because the process reminded him too clearly of what he had been doing in Whitechapel? Did he retire from UCH and the other places in which he worked because he no longer wanted temptation, in the form of poor and compliant women patients, to be placed before him? Did he stop speaking and writing at the Obstetrical Society because he no longer had the confidence to do so after he had proved to himself that he was flawed, flawed in his intelligence and flawed in his morals?

In the next couple of years John Williams made changes to his life that remained for the rest of his days. Once he moved down to Plas Llanstephan, he only returned to the world of medicine to attend meetings of the General Medical Council, and to help out at the birth of Princess Mary's children. The years in Harley Street, in Queen Anne Street, and latterly Brook Street, paid off as he enjoyed a comfortable retirement and indulged himself in collecting the vast numbers of books that he was later to donate to the National Library of Wales. Of the years in Whitechapel, perhaps there were only a few small reminders; some microscopic slides, a knife, a letter or two, and the odd reminder in his papers, such as the notation of his meeting with the patient Mary Ann Nichols. And his diary for 1888, its pages carefully but systematically removed.

In June 1903 a banquet was held in Cardiff, at the Royal Hotel, in honour of Sir John Williams, to mark his retirement and return to Wales. Present at the banquet were dignitaries from the city and from the surrounding area, among them many medical men. Perhaps most moving for the doctor was the presence of his old employer, Dr Ebenezer Davies, who not only came to the dinner, along with dozens of others, but also spoke in praise of his former employee. Sir John was pleased to especially thank Dr Davies, 'who had given him his start in the medical profession and bestowed upon him much valued advice'. The following was recorded in the *Lancet* of that month:

> Some while ago he had been asked by one of the newspapers which enjoyed a large circulation to give its columns some of his reminiscences. He felt that these were such as could not appear in such circumstances. And so in expressing his gratification at the sentiments which were manifested towards him he must now confine himself to his very sincere acknowledgements.

It is not in the least surprising that John Williams refused to record his 'reminiscences' for the public, even if it was for a paper 'with a large circulation'. Of course he would not want to record his past in public; it was interesting that he could not even risk a sanitised version in front of those who were honouring him. As we had surmised, John Williams dared not look back into his past in London. It was too unsettling to acknowledge what he had done, even if he had been able to justify it to himself at the time; consequently he chose instead to ignore it.

He had turned his back on medicine, he had turned his back on London, he had now turned his back on his own history. Were it possible to erase all evidence of his past life, he would have done so, but he had taken what precautions he could, and now it was down to his manipulation of the future. If he could only ensure that the right legacy was what remained – the National Library of Wales, in Aberystwyth – then the events of Whitechapel in 1888 would never be associated with him.

Epilogue

Wandering around some of the sites that are now associated with John Williams – not just those in Swansea, or the National Library of Wales, but also the student halls on the seafront of Aberystwyth, named after the man, and of course the larger buildings and institutions such as University College Hospital and the Royal Society of Obstetricians and Gynaecologists – it is hard not to feel a twinge of guilt. Guilt for the fact that this man's name would always be coupled with something other than the great works of book-collecting and abdominal operations with which he is now associated. Whatever the wider world would come to believe of his story, the places linked to John Williams would never be quite the same again.

One day we would like to return to the National Library of Wales with more than just notebooks. The three microscopic slides with something on them and the knife, that rest in their vaults, may yet reveal one last secret. Would the opportunity to use a microscope, in the company of someone who knew what to look for, show us that this is the last remaining evidence of the lives of the victims in Whitechapel? Is it possible that on the blade of the knife, or under the glass of the slides, there remain traces of DNA that could confirm our suspicions? And even if there were traces on them, after a gap of over a hundred and seventeen years, what would we test them against?

Next door to the library is the Aberystwyth branch of the University of Wales. It is a thriving place, and the legacy of John Williams rests in his name adorning some halls and a chair within one of the schools. The money he left it is presumably long spent. University College Hospital is in the middle of a multimillion pound rebuilding programme. The obstetric department, in Gower Street, where John Williams worked, is now converted into offices.

Sir John Williams, 'a man of yeoman and non-conformist stock', died in May 1926. Large numbers of the town's dignitaries turned out for his funeral. In his will, he left over £100,000 to the National Library and to the University in Aberystwyth, and nothing to his family. 'The library ... will ever remain as the memorial of a far-seeing and single-minded man,' said the *Lancet*, in his obituary. We went to visit Sir John's grave in Aberystwyth. It is in the centre of a large cemetery, not too grand, and not too well cared for, but he is buried alongside his wife. Above the town stands his real monument; the overly grand and monolithic building of the National Library of Wales, the house that Jack built.

The Ripper's victims were buried in graves in East London. It is possible today to visit some of the sites, but others are gone – buried in unmarked pauper's graves. The inquests into their deaths recorded 'wilful murder by some person unknown'.

Bibliography

The Complete History of Jack the Ripper, Philip Sugden (London, 2002)

Jack the Ripper A–Z, Paul Begg, Martin Fido and Keith Skinner (London, 1996)

The Complete Jack the Ripper, Donald Rumbelow (London, 1987)

The Mammoth Book of Jack the Ripper, eds Maxim Jakubowski and Nathan Braund (London, 1999)

Jack the Ripper: the Final Chapter, Paul H. Feldman (London, 1998)

From Hell, Alan Moore (London, 2000)

'The Whitechapel Murders: the Case of Jack the Ripper', W.G. Eckert, *American Journal of Forensic Medicine and Pathology*, Vol. II, No.1 (March, 1981)

Life and Labour, Vol. I: East London, Charles Booth (London, 1889)

Women Under the Knife: a History of Surgery, Ann Dally (London, 1991)

The Medical Profession in Mid-Victorian London, M. Jeanne Peterson (Berkeley and Los Angeles, 1978)

The Workhouse System, 1834-1929: the History of an English Social Institution, A.J. Crowther (London, 1981)

'Joseph Rogers and the Reform of Workhouse Medicine', Ruth Richardson and Brian Horwitz (*History Workshop*, 43, 1997)

The Development of the London Hospital System, 1823-1982, Geoffrey Rivett (London, 1986)

Death, Dissection and the Destitute, Ruth Richardson, (2nd edition, London, 2001)

The National Medical Dictionary, S.S. Billings (Edinburgh and London, 1890)

Kimpson's Pocket Medical Dictionary, Thomas Dutton (London, 1907)

The Worm in the Bud: the World of Victorian Sexuality, Ronald Pearsall (Harmondsworth, 1971)

Historical Review of British Obstetrics and Gynaecology, 1800-1950, eds J.M. Munro-Kerr, R.W. Johnstone, Miles H. Phillips (Edinburgh and London, 1954)

Lost London: the Memoirs of an East-End Detective, by Ex-Det. Sergeant B. Leeson (London, 1934)

East End 1888, William J. Fishman (London, 1988)

The Lloyd George I Knew, Sir Alfred T. Davies (London, 1948)

I Caught Crippen; Memoirs of Ex-Chief Inspector Walter Dew, CID, Walter Dew *(London, 1938)*

The Autobiography of Margot Asquith, ed. Mark Bonham Carter (London, 1962)

The Asquiths, Colin Clifford (London, 2002)

Born in the Blood: the Lost Secrets of Freemasonry, John J. Robinson (London, 1989)

The Passport: the History of Man's Most Travelled Document, Martin Lloyd (Gloucester, 2003)

A Letter on Some Matters of Poor Law Administration, Addressed (With Permission) to the Rt Hon. The President of the Local Government Board, Louisa Twining (London, 1887)

A History of Modern Wales, David William (London, 1950)

Y Cymmrodor, Embodying the Transaction of the Honourable Society of Cymmrodorion, ed. Thomas Powel, Vol. VII, pt I (London, 1884), Vol. VIII, pt II (London, 1887)

Sir John Williams, 1840-1926, Ruth Evans (Cardiff, 1952)

The National Library of Wales: a Survey of its History, its Contents, and its Activities, W.L.L. Davies (Aberystwyth, 1937)

A Refuge in Peace and War: the National Library of Wales to

1952, David Jenkins (Aberystwyth, 2002)

'Twenty Fourteen': a History of the South Wales Tinplate Industry, 1700-1961, Paul Jenkins (Dyfed, 1995)

University College Hospital and its Medical School, W.R. Merrington (London, 1976)

'Obituary of Sir John Williams', Herbert Spencer, *University College Hospital Magazine*, Vol. XV (September, 1926)

'The Medical Aspect of the Life of Sir John Williams', Iowerth Hughes Jones, *National Library of Wales Journal*, Vol. IX/2 (Winter, 1955)

'Sir John Williams Centenary', *National Library of Wales Journal*, Vol. I/4 (Winter, 1940)

'Sir John Williams: His Background and Achievement', Emyr Wyn Jones, *Wales and Medicine: an Historical Survey, From Papers Given at the Ninth British Congress on the History of Medicine, at Swansea and Cardiff, 4-8 September 1973*, ed. John Cule (London)

Sources

Our thanks to the Librarian and staff at the following institutions for their assistance and assiduous attention to detail, and our apologies for not being able to tell them *exactly* what it was that we wanted to know about John Williams:

The National Library of Wales, Aberystwyth
The Wellcome Library, London
The Archives and Museum at the Royal London Hospital, Whitechapel, London
The British Library, Euston
The British Library (Newspapers) at Colindale
The London Metropolitan Archives
The Royal Society of Obstetricians and Gynaecologists
University College Hospital Archive
Bodleian Library, Oxford
The Archives of Her Majesty the Queen at Windsor Castle
RA Queen Victoria's Journal, 22 November 1886
RA King George V's Diary: 21 July 1905

Michael Phelps, archivist at West Glamorgan Archives Centre, County Hall, Swansea.

WEBSITES
The most comprehensive resource on the internet, encompassing everything related to Jack the Ripper, is the excellent Casebook: Jack the Ripper, www.casebook.org

Index